CAPE EDITIONS 29

General Editor: NATHANIEL TARN

Soul on Ice
Eldridge Cleaver

JONATHAN CAPE
THIRTY BEDFORD SQUARE
LONDON

First published in Great Britain 1969
Reprinted 1969 (3 times), 1970 (twice), 1971 (twice)

Copyright © 1968 by Eldridge Cleaver

Jonathan Cape Ltd, 30 Bedford Square, London, WC1

ISBN Paperback edition 0 224 61551 3
    Hardback edition 0 224 61552 1

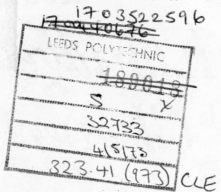
Condition of Sale

This book is sold subject to the condition that it shall not,
by way of trade or otherwise, be lent, re-sold, hired out,
or otherwise circulated without the publisher's prior consent
in any form of binding or cover other than that in which
it is published and without a similar condition including this
condition being imposed on the subsequent purchaser.

Printed and bound in Great Britain
by Richard Clay (The Chaucer Press) Ltd,
Bungay, Suffolk

Contents

To Beverly, with whom I share
the ultimate of love

ACKNOWLEDGMENTS

Of all the beautiful people who have been so helpful in getting these writings into print, I'd like to thank especially Edward M. Keating, creator of *Ramparts* magazine, who was the first professional to pay any attention to my writings; Maxwell Geismar, whose criticism has helped me gain a degree of control over my materials; and David Welsh, for his invaluable assistance as an editor.

Acknowledgment is also made to the following sources for permission to quote from material already published:

The Dead Lecturer by LeRoi Jones (The Sterling Lord Agency, 1964)

The Natural Superiority of Women by Ashley Montagu (Collier/Macmillan, 1953)

'My Negro Problem – and Ours' by Norman Podhoretz (*Commentary*, 1963)

A letter by Irving Louis Horowitz (*Commentary*, 1963)

The Presidential Papers by Norman Mailer (André Deutsch, 1964)

The Fire Next Time by James Baldwin (Michael Joseph, 1963)

On the Road by Jack Kerouac (André Deutsch, 1958)

Part One

LETTERS FROM PRISON

ON BECOMING

Folsom Prison,
June 25th, 1965

Nineteen fifty-four, when I was eighteen years old, is held to be a crucial turning point in the history of the Afro-American – for the U.S.A. as a whole – the year segregation was outlawed by the U.S. Supreme Court. It was also a crucial year for me because on June 18th, 1954, I began serving a sentence in state prison for possession of marijuana.

The Supreme Court decision was only one month old when I entered prison, and I do not believe that I had even the vaguest idea of its importance or historical significance. But later, the acrimonious controversy ignited by the end of the separate-but-equal doctrine was to have a profound effect on me. This controversy awakened me to my position in America and I began to form a concept of what it meant to be black in white America.

Of course I'd always known that I was black, but I'd never really stopped to take stock of what I was involved in. I met life as an individual and took my chances. Prior to 1954, we lived in an atmosphere of novocain. Negroes found it necessary, in order to maintain whatever sanity they could, to remain somewhat aloof and detached from 'the problem'. We accepted indignities and the mechanics of the apparatus of oppression without reacting by sitting-in or holding mass demonstrations. Nurtured by the fires of the controversy over segregation, I was soon aflame with indignation over my newly discovered social status, and inwardly I turned away from America with horror, disgust and outrage.

In Soledad state prison, I fell in with a group of young blacks who, like myself, were in vociferous rebellion against what we perceived as a continuation of slavery on a higher plane. We cursed everything American – including baseball and hot dogs. All respect we may have had for politicians, preachers, lawyers, governors, Presidents, senators, congressmen was utterly destroyed as we watched them temporizing and compromising over right and wrong, over legality and illegality, over constitutionality and unconstitutionality. We knew that in the end what they were clashing over was us, what to do with the blacks, and whether or not to start treating us as human beings. I despised all of them.

The segregationists were condemned out of hand, without even listening to their lofty, finely woven arguments. The others I despised for wasting time in debates with the segregationists: why not just crush them, put them in prison – they were defying the law, weren't they? I defied the law and they put me in prison. So why not put those dirty mothers in prison too? I had gotten caught with a shopping bag full of marijuana, a shopping bag full of love – I was in love with the weed and I did not for one minute think that anything was wrong with getting high. I had been getting high for four or five years and was convinced, with the zeal of a crusader, that marijuana was superior to lush – yet the rulers of the land seemed all to be lushes. I could not see how they were more justified in drinking than I was in blowing the gage. I was a grasshopper, and it was natural that I felt myself to be unjustly imprisoned.

While all this was going on, our group was espousing atheism. Unsophisticated and not based on any philosophical rationale, our atheism was pragmatic. I had come to believe that there is no God; if there is, men do not know anything about him. Therefore, all religions were phony – which made all preachers and priests, in our eyes, fakers, including the ones scurrying around the prison who, curiously, could put in a good word for you with the Almighty Creator of the universe but could not get anything down with the warden or parole board – they could usher you through the Pearly Gates *after you were dead*, but not through the prison gate *while you were still alive and kicking*. Besides, men of the cloth who work in prison have an ineradicable stigma attached to them in the eyes of convicts because they escort condemned men into the gas chamber. Such men of God are powerful arguments in favor of atheism. Our atheism was a source of enormous pride to me. Later on, I bolstered our arguments by reading Thomas Paine and his devastating critique of Christianity in particular and organized religion in general.

Through reading I was amazed to discover how confused people were. I had thought that, out there beyond the horizon of my own ignorance, unanimity existed, that even though I myself didn't know what was happening in the universe, other people certainly did. Yet here I was discovering that the whole U.S.A. was in a chaos of disagreement over segregation/ integration. In these circumstances I decided that the only safe thing for me to do was go for myself. It became clear that it was possible for me to take the initiative: instead of simply *reacting* I could *act*. I could unilaterally – whether anyone agreed with me or not – repudiate all allegiances, morals, values – even while continuing to exist within this society. My mind would be free and no power in the universe could force me to accept something if I didn't want to. But I would take my own sweet time. That, too, was a part of my new freedom. I would accept nothing until it was proved that it was good – for me. I became an extreme iconoclast. Any affirmative assertion made by anyone around me became a target for tirades of criticism and denunciation.

This little game got good to me and I got good at it. I attacked all forms of piety, loyalty and sentiment: marriage, love, God, patriotism, the Constitution, the founding fathers, law, concepts of right-wrong-good-evil, all forms of ritualized and conventional behavior. As I pranced about, club in hand, seeking new idols to smash, I encountered really for the first time in my life, with any seriousness, The Ogre, rising up before me in a mist. I discovered, with alarm, that The Ogre possessed a tremendous and dreadful power over me, and I didn't understand this power or why I was at its mercy. I tried to repudiate The Ogre, root it out of my heart as I had done God, Constitution, principles, morals, and values – but The Ogre had its claws buried in the core of my being and refused to let go. I fought frantically to be free, but The Ogre only mocked me and sank its claws deeper into my soul. I knew then that I had found an important key, that if I conquered The Ogre and broke its power over me I would be free. But I also knew that it was a race against time and that if I did not win I would certainly be broken and destroyed. I, a black man, confronted The Ogre – the white woman.

In prison, those things withheld from and denied to the prisoner become precisely what he wants most of all, of course. Because we were locked up in our cells before darkness fell, I used to lie awake at night racked by painful craving to take a leisurely stroll under the stars, or to go to the beach, to drive a car on a freeway, to grow a beard, or to make love to a woman.

Since I was not married conjugal visits would not have solved my problem. I therefore denounced the idea of conjugal visits as inherently unfair; single prisoners needed and deserved *action* just as married prisoners did. I advocated establishing a system under Civil Service whereby salaried women would minister to the needs of those prisoners who maintained a record of good behavior. If a married prisoner preferred his own wife, that would be his right. Since California was not about to inaugurate either conjugal visits or the Civil Service, one could advocate either with equal enthusiasm and with the same result: nothing.

This may appear ridiculous to some people. But it was very real to me and as urgent as the need to breathe, because I was in my bull stage and lack of access to females was absolutely a form of torture. I suffered. My mistress at the time of my arrest, the beautiful and lonely wife of a serviceman stationed overseas, died unexpectedly three weeks after I entered prison; and the rigid, dehumanized rules governing correspondence between prisoners and free people prevented me from corresponding with other young ladies I knew. It left me without any contact with females except those in my family.

In the process of enduring my confinement, I decided to get myself a pin-up girl to paste on the wall of my cell. I would fall in love with her and lavish my affections upon her. She, a symbolic representative of the forbidden tribe of women, would sustain me until I was free. Out of the center of *Esquire*, I married a voluptuous bride. Our marriage went along swell for a time: no quarrels, no complaints. And then, one evening when I came in from school, I was shocked and enraged to find that the guard had entered my cell, ripped my sugar from the wall, torn her into little pieces, and left the pieces floating in the commode: it was like seeing a dead body floating in a lake. Giving her a proper burial, I flushed the commode. As the saying goes, I sent her to Long Beach. But I was genuinely beside myself with anger: almost every cell, excepting those of the homo-sexuals, had a pin-up girl on the wall and the guards didn't bother them. Why, I asked the guard the next day, had he singled me out for special treatment?

'Don't you know we have a rule against pasting up pictures on the walls?' he asked me.

'Later for the rules,' I said. 'You know as well as I do that that rule is not enforced.'

'Tell you what,' he said, smiling at me (the smile put me on my guard), 'I'll compromise with you: get yourself a colored girl for a pin-up – no white women – and I'll let it stay up. Is that a deal?'

I was more embarrassed than shocked. He was laughing in my face. I called him two or three dirty names and walked away. I can still recall his big moon-face, grinning at me over yellow teeth. The disturbing part about the whole incident was that a terrible feeling of guilt came over me as I realized that I had chosen the picture of the white girl over the available pictures of black girls. I tried to rational-ize it away, but I was fascinated by the truth involved.

Why hadn't I thought about it in this light before? So I took hold of the question and began to inquire into my feelings. Was it true, did I really prefer white girls over black? The conclusion was clear and inescapable: I did. I decided to check out my friends on this point and it was easy to determine, from listening to their general conversation, that the white woman occupied a peculiarly prominent place in all of our frames of reference. With what I have learned since then, this all seems terribly elementary now. But at the time, it was a tremendously intriguing adventure of discovery.

One afternoon, when a large group of Negroes was on the prison yard shooting the breeze, I grabbed the floor and posed the question: which did they prefer, white women or black? Some said Japanese women were their favorite, others said Chinese, some said European women, others said Mexican women – they all stated a preference, and they generally freely admitted their dislike for black women.

'I don't want nothing black but a Cadillac,' said one.

'If money was black I wouldn't want none of it,' put in another.

A short little stud, who was a very good lightweight boxer with a little man's complex that made him love to box heavyweights, jumped to his feet. He had a yellowish complexion and we called him Butterfly.

'All you niggers are sick!' Butterfly spat out. 'I don't like no stinking white woman. My grandma is a white woman and I don't even like her!'

But it just so happened that Butterfly's crime partner was in the crowd, and after Butterfly had his say, his crime partner said, 'Aw, sit down and quit that lying, lil o' chump. What about that gray girl in San

Jose who had your nose wide open? Did you like her, or were you just running after her with your tongue hanging out of your head because you hated her?'

Partly because he was embarrassed and partly because his crime partner was a heavyweight, Butterfly flew into him. And before we could separate them and disperse, so the guard would not know who had been fighting, Butterfly bloodied his crime partner's nose. Butterfly got away but, because of the blood, his crime partner got caught. I ate dinner with Butterfly that evening and questioned him sharply about his attitude toward white women. And after an initial evasiveness he admitted that the white woman bugged him too. 'It's a sickness,' he said. 'All our lives we've had the white woman dangled before our eyes like a carrot on a stick before a donkey: look but don't touch.' (In 1958, after I had gone out on parole and was returned to San Quentin as a parole violater with a new charge, Butterfly was still there. He had become a Black Muslim and was chiefly responsible for teaching me the Black Muslim philosophy. Upon his release from San Quentin, Butterfly joined the Los Angeles Mosque, advanced rapidly through the ranks, and is now a full-fledged minister of one of Elijah Muhammad's mosques in another city. He successfully completed his parole, got married – to a very black girl – and is doing fine.)

From our discussion, which began that evening and has never yet ended, we went on to notice how thoroughly, as a matter of course, a black growing up in America is indoctrinated with the white race's standard of beauty. Not that the whites made a conscious, calculated effort to do this, we thought, but since they constituted the majority the whites brainwashed the blacks by the very processes the whites employed to indoctrinate themselves with their own group standards. It intensified my frustrations to know that I was indoctrinated to see the white woman as more beautiful and desirable than my own black woman. It drove me into books seeking light on the subject. In Richard Wright's *Native Son*, I found Bigger Thomas and a keen insight into the problem.

My interest in this area persisted undiminished and then, in 1955, an event took place in Mississippi which turned me inside out: Emmett Till, a young Negro down from Chicago on a visit, was murdered, allegedly for flirting with a white woman. He had been shot, his head crushed from repeated blows with a blunt instrument, and his badly decomposed body was recovered from the river with a heavy weight on it. I was, of course, angry over the whole bit, but one day I saw in a magazine a picture of the white woman with whom Emmett Till was said to have flirted. While looking at the picture, I felt that little tension in the center of my chest I experience when a woman appeals to me. I was disgusted and angry with myself. Here was a woman who had caused the death of a black, possibly because, when he looked at her, he also felt the same tensions of lust and desire in his chest – and probably for the same general reasons that I felt them. It was all unacceptable to me. I looked at the picture again and again, and in spite of everything and against my will and the hate I felt for the woman and all that she represented, she appealed to me. I flew into a rage at myself, at America, at white women, at the history that had placed those tensions of lust and desire in my chest.

Two days later I had a 'nervous breakdown'. For several days I ranted and raved against the white race, against white women in particular, against white America in general. When I came to myself, I was locked in a padded cell with not even the vaguest memory of how I got there. All I could recall was an eternity of pacing back and forth in the cell, preaching to the unhearing walls.

I had several sessions with a psychiatrist. His conclusion was that I hated my mother. How he arrived at this conclusion I'll never know, because he knew nothing about my mother; and when he'd ask me questions I would answer him with absurd lies. What revolted me about him was that he had heard me denouncing the whites, yet each time he interviewed me he deliberately guided the conversation back to my family life, to my childhood. That in itself was all right, but he deliberately blocked all my attempts to bring out the racial question, and he made it clear that he was not interested in my attitude toward whites. This was a Pandora's box he did not care to open. After I ceased my diatribes against the whites, I was let out of the hospital, back into the general inmate population just as if nothing had happened. I continued to brood over these events and over the dynamics of race relations in America.

During this period I was concentrating my reading in the field of economics. Having previously dabbled in the theories and writings of Rousseau, Thomas Paine, and Voltaire, I had added a little polish to my iconoclastic stance, without, however, bothering too much to understand their affirmative positions. In economics, because everybody seemed to find it necessary to attack and condemn Karl Marx in their writings, I sought out his books, and although he kept me with a headache, I took him for my authority. I was not prepared to understand him, but I was able to see in him a thoroughgoing critique and condemnation of capitalism. It was like taking medicine for me to find that, indeed, American capitalism deserved all the hatred and contempt that I felt for it in my heart. This had a positive, stabilizing effect upon me – to an extent because I was not about to become stable – and it diverted me from my previous preoccupation: morbid broodings on the black man and the white woman. Pursuing my readings into the history of socialism, I read, with very little understanding, some of the passionate, exhortatory writings of Lenin; and I fell in love with Bakunin and Nechayev's *Catechism of the Revolutionist* – the principles of which, along with some of Machiavelli's advice, I sought to incorporate into my own behavior. I took the *Catechism* for my bible and, standing on a one-man platform that had nothing to do with the reconstruction of society, I began consciously incorporating these principles into my daily life, to employ tactics of ruthlessness in my dealings with everyone with whom I came into contact. And I began to look at white America through these new eyes.

Somehow I arrived at the conclusion that, as a matter of principle, it was of paramount importance for me to have an antagonistic, ruthless attitude toward white women. The term *outlaw* appealed to me and at the time my parole date was drawing near, I considered myself to be mentally free – I was an 'outlaw'. I had stepped outside of the white man's law, which I repudiated with scorn and self-satisfaction. I became a law unto myself – my own legislature, my own supreme court, my own executive. At the moment I walked out of the prison gate, my feelings toward white women in general could be summed up in the following lines:

TO A WHITE GIRL

I love you
Because you're white,
Not because you're charming
Or bright.
Your whiteness
Is a silky thread
Snaking through my thoughts
In redhot patterns
Of lust and desire.

I hate you
Because you're white.
Your white meat
Is nightmare food.
White is
The skin of Evil.
You're my Moby Dick,
White Witch,
Symbol of the rope and hanging tree,
Of the burning cross.
Loving you thus
And hating you so,
My heart is torn in two.
Crucified.

I became a rapist. To refine my technique and
modus operandi, I started out by practicing on black
girls in the ghetto – in the black ghetto where dark
and vicious deeds appear not as aberrations or devia-
tions from the norm, but as part of the sufficiency
of the Evil of a day – and when I considered myself
smooth enough, I crossed the tracks and sought out
white prey. I did this consciously, deliberately, will-
fully, methodically – though looking back I see that

I was in a frantic, wild, and completely abandoned frame of mind.

Rape was an insurrectionary act. It delighted me that I was defying and trampling upon the white man's law, upon his system of values, and that I was defiling his women – and this point, I believe, was the most satisfying to me because I was very resentful over the historical fact of how the white man has used the black woman. I felt I was getting revenge. From the site of the act of rape, consternation spreads outwardly in concentric circles. I wanted to send waves of consternation throughout the white race. Recently, I came upon a quotation from one of LeRoi Jones's poems, taken from his book *The Dead Lecturer* :

A cult of death need of the simple striking arm
under the street lamp. The cutters from under
their rented earth. Come up, black dada nihilis-
mus. Rape the white girls. Rape their fathers.
Cut the mothers' throats.

I have lived those lines and I know that if I had not been apprehended I would have slit some white throats. There are, of course, many young blacks out there right now who are slitting white throats and raping the white girl. They are not doing this because they read LeRoi Jones's poetry, as some of his critics seem to believe. Rather, LeRoi is expressing the funky facts of life.

After I returned to prison, I took a long look at myself and, for the first time in my life, admitted that I was wrong, that I had gone astray – astray not so much from the white man's law as from being human, civilized – for I could not approve the act of rape. Even though I had some insight into my own motivations, I did not feel justified. I lost my self-respect. My pride as a man dissolved and my whole fragile moral structure seemed to collapse, completely shattered.

That is why I started to write. To save myself.

I realized that no one could save me but myself. The prison authorities were both uninterested and unable to help me. I had to seek out the truth and unravel the snarled web of my motivations. I had to find out who I am and what I want to be, what type of man I should be, and what I could do to become the best of which I was capable. I understood that what had happened to me had also happened to countless other blacks and it would happen to many, many more.

I learned that I had been taking the easy way out, running away from problems. I also learned that it is easier to do evil than it is to do good. And I have been terribly impressed by the youth of America, black and white. I am proud of them because they have reaffirmed my faith in humanity. I have come to feel what must be love for the young people of America and I want to be part of the good and greatness that they want for all people. From my prison cell, I have watched America slowly coming awake. It is not fully awake yet, but there is soul in the air and everywhere I see beauty. I have watched the sit-ins, the freedom rides the Mississippi Blood Summers, demonstrations all over the country, the F.S.M. movement, the teach-ins, and the mounting protest over Lyndon Strangelove's foreign policy – all of this, the thousands of little details, show me it is time to straighten up and fly right. That is why I decided to concentrate on my writings and efforts in this area. We are a very sick country – I, perhaps, am sicker than most. But

I accept that. I told you in the beginning that I am extremist by nature – so it is only right that I should be extremely sick.

I was very familiar with the Eldridge who came to prison, but that Eldridge no longer exists. And the one I am now is in some ways a stranger to me. You may find this difficult to understand but it is very easy for one in prison to lose his sense of self. And if he has been undergoing all kinds of extreme, involved, and unregulated changes, then he ends up not knowing who he is. Take the point of being attractive to women. You can easily see how a man can lose his arrogance or certainty on that point while in prison! When he's in the free world, he gets constant feedback on how he looks from the number of female heads he turns when he walks down the street. In prison he gets only hatestares and sour frowns. Years and years of bitter looks. Individuality is not nourished in prison, neither by the officials nor by the convicts. It is a deep hole out of which to climb.

What must be done, I believe, is that all these problems – particularly the sickness between the white woman and the black man – must be brought out into the open, dealt with and resolved. I know that the black man's sick attitude toward the white woman is a revolutionary sickness: it keeps him perpetually out of harmony with the system that is oppressing him. Many whites flatter themselves with the idea that the Negro male's lust and desire for the white dream girl is purely an esthetic attraction, but nothing could be further from the truth. His motivation is often of such a bloody, hateful, bitter, and malignant nature that whites would really be hard pressed to find it flattering. I have discussed these points with prisoners who were convicted of rape, and their motivations are very plain. But they are very reluctant to discuss these things with white men who, by and large, make up the prison staffs. I believe that in the experience of these men lies the knowledge and wisdom that must be utilized to help other youngsters who are heading in the same direction. I think all of us, the entire nation, will be better off if we bring it all out front. A lot of people's feelings will be hurt, but that is the price that must be paid.

It may be that I can harm myself by speaking frankly and directly, but I do not care about that at all. Of course I want to get out of prison, badly, but I shall get out some day. I am more concerned with what I am going to be after I get out. I know that by following the course which I have charted I will find my salvation. If I had followed the path laid down for me by the officials, I'd undoubtedly have long since been out of prison – but I'd be less of a man. I'd be weaker and less certain of where I want to go, what I want to do, and how to go about it.

The price of hating other human beings is loving oneself less.

SOUL ON ICE

Folsom Prison,
October 9th, 1965

I'm perfectly aware that I'm in prison, that I'm a
Negro, that I've been a rapist, and that I have a
Higher Uneducation. I never know what significance
I'm supposed to attach to these factors. But I have a
suspicion that, because of these aspects of my
character, 'free-normal-educated' people rather expect
me to be more reserved, penitent, remorseful, and not
too quick to shoot off my mouth on certain subjects.
But I let them down, disappoint them, make them
gape at me in a sort of stupor, as if they're thinking :
'You've got your nerve! Don't you realize that you
owe a debt to society?' My answer to all such
thoughts lurking in their split-level heads, crouching
behind their squinting bombardier eyes, is that the
blood of Vietnamese peasants has paid off all my
debts; that the Vietnamese people, afflicted with a
rampant disease called Yankees, through their suffer-
ings – as opposed to the 'frustration' of fat-assed
American geeks safe at home worrying over whether
to have bacon, ham, or sausage with their grade-A
eggs in the morning, while Vietnamese worry each
morning whether the Yankees will gas them, burn
them up, or blow away their humble pads in a hail
of bombs – have canceled all my I.O.U.s.

In beginning this letter I could just as easily have

mentioned other aspects of my situation; I could have said: I'm perfectly aware that I'm tall, that I'm skinny, that I need a shave, that I'm hard-up enough to suck my grandmother's old withered tits, and that I would dig (deeper than deeply) getting *clean* once more – not only in the steam-bath sense, but in getting sharp as an *Esquire* square with a Harlem touch – or that I would like to put on a pair of bib overalls and become a Snicker, or that I'd like to leap the whole last mile and grow a beard and don whatever threads the local nationalism might require and comrade with Che Guevara, and share his fate, blazing a new pathfinder's trail through the stymied upbeat brain of the New Left, or how I'd just love to be in Berkeley right now, to roll in that mud, frolic in that sty of funky revolution, to breathe in its heady fumes, and look with roving eyes for a new John Brown, Eugene Debs, a blacker-meaner-keener Malcolm X, a Robert Franklin Williams with less rabbit in his hot blood, an American Lenin, Fidel, a Mao-Mao, A MAO MAO, A MAO MAO, A MAO MAO, A MAO MAO, A MAO MAO, A MAO MAO ... All of which is true.

But what matters is that I have fallen in love with my lawyer! Is that surprising? A convict is expected to have a high regard for *anyone* who comes to his aid, who tries to help him and who expends time, energy, and money in an effort to set him free. But can a convict really love a lawyer? It goes against the grain. Convicts hate lawyers. To walk around a prison yard and speak well of a lawyer is to raise the downcast eyebrows of felons who've been bitten by members of the Bar and Grill. Convicts are convinced that lawyers must have a secret little black book which no one else is ever allowed to see, a book that school lawyers in an esoteric morality in which

the Highest Good is treachery and crossing one's
dumb and trusting client the noblest of deeds. It was
learned by the convicts that I'd gotten busted with
some magazines given to me by my lawyer and that
I was thrown in the Hole for it. Convicts smiled
knowingly and told me that I had gone for the
greasy pig, that my lawyer had set me up, and that
if I couldn't see through the plot I was so stupid that
I would buy not only the Golden Gate Bridge but
some fried ice cream.

It was my turn to smile knowingly. A convict's
paranoia is as thick as the prison wall – and just as
necessary. Why should we have faith in anyone?
Even our wives and lovers whose beds we have shared,
with whom we have shared the tenderest moments
and most delicate relations, leave us after a while,
put us down, cut us clean aloose and treat us like they
hate us, won't even write us a letter, send us a Christ-
mas card every other year, or a quarter for a pack of
cigarettes or a tube of toothpaste now and then. All
society shows the convict its ass and expects him to
kiss it: the convict feels like kicking it or putting a
bullet in it. A convict sees man's fangs and claws and
learns quickly to bare and unsheath his own, for real
and final. To maintain a hold on the ideals and senti-
ments of civilization in such circumstances is probably impossible. How much more incredible is it,
then, while rooted in this pit, to fall in love, and
with a lawyer! Use a lawyer, yes: use anybody. Even
tell the lawyer that you're in love. But you will
always know when you are lying and even if you
could manage to fool the lawyer you could never
manage to fool yourself.

And why does it make you sad to see how everything hangs by such thin and whimsical threads?

Because you're a dreamer, an incredible dreamer, with a tiny spark hidden somewhere inside you which cannot die, which even you cannot kill or quench and which tortures you horribly because all the odds are against its continual burning. In the midst of the foulest decay and putrid savagery, this spark speaks to you of beauty, of human warmth and kindness, of goodness, of greatness, of heroism, of martyrdom, and it speaks to you of love.

So I love my lawyer. My lawyer is not an ordinary person. My lawyer is a rebel, a revolutionary who is alienated fundamentally from the *status quo*, probably with as great an intensity, conviction, and irretrievability as I am alienated from it – and probably with more intelligence, compassion, and humanity. If you read the papers, you are no doubt aware of my lawyer's incessant involvement in agitation against all manifestations of the monstrous evil of our system, such as our intervention in the internal affairs of the Vietnamese people or the invasion of the Dominican Republic by U.S. Marines. And my lawyer defends civil rights demonstrators, sit-iners, and the Free Speech students who rebelled against the Kerr–Strong machine at the University of California. My love for my lawyer is due, in part, to these activities and involvements, because we are always on the same side of the issues. And I love all my allies. But this, which may be the beginning of an explanation, does not nearly explain what goes on between my lawyer and me.

I suppose that I should be honest and, before going any further, admit that my lawyer is a woman – or maybe I should have held back with that piece of the puzzle – a very excellent, unusual, and beautiful woman. I know that *she* believes that I do not really love her and that I am confusing a combination of lust and gratitude for love. Lust and gratitude I feel abundantly, but I also love this woman. And I fear that, believing that I do not love her, she will act according to that belief.

At night, I talk with her in my sleep, long dialogues in which she answers back. We alternate in speaking, like in the script of a play. And let me say that I don't believe a word she says. While we are talking, I participate and believe everything, taking her word as her bond. But when I awake, I repudiate the conversation and disbelieve her. I awake refreshed, and though my sleep has been restless, I am not tired. Except for a few lost hours in which she slips away and I fall into a deep sleep, I hover on a level between consciousness and peace, and the dialogue ensues. It does not bother me now. I have often gone through this when something seizes my mind.

I place a great deal of emphasis on people really listening to each other, to what the other person has to say, because you very seldom encounter a person who is capable of taking either you or himself seriously. Of course, when I was out of prison I was not really like this; the seeds were there, but there was too much confusion and madness mixed in. I had a profound desire for communicating with and getting to know other people, but I was incapable of doing so. I didn't know how.

Getting to know someone, entering that new world, is an ultimate, irretrievable leap into the unknown. The prospect is terrifying. The stakes are high. The emotions are overwhelming. The two people are reluctant really to strip themselves naked in front of each other, because in doing so they make themselves vulnerable and give enormous power over themselves

c

one to the other. How often they inflict pain and torment upon each other! Better to maintain shallow, superficial affairs; that way the scars are not too deep. No blood is hacked from the soul.

But I do not believe a beautiful relationship has to end always in carnage, or that we have to be fraudulent and pretentious with one another. If we project fraudulent, pretentious images, or if we fantasize each other into distorted caricatures of what we really are, then, when we awake from the trance and see beyond the sham and front, all will dissolve, all will die or be transformed into bitterness and hate. I know that sometimes people fake on each other out of genuine motives to hold on to the object of their tenderest feelings. They see themselves as so inadequate that they feel forced to wear a mask in order continuously to impress the second party.

If a man is free – not in prison, the army, a monastery, hospital, spaceship, submarine – and living a normal life with the usual multiplicity of social relations with individuals of both sexes, it may be that he is incapable of experiencing the total impact of another individual upon himself. The competing influences and conflicting forces of other personalities may dilute one's psychic and emotional perception, to the extent that one does not and cannot receive all that the other person is capable of sending.

Yet I may believe that a man whose soul or emotional apparatus had lain dormant in a deadening limbo of desuetude is capable of responding from some great sunken well of his being, as though a potent catalyst had been tossed into a critical mass, when an exciting, lovely, and lovable woman enters the range of his feelings. What a deep, slow, tortuous, reluctant, frightened stirring! He feels a certain part of himself in a state of flux, as if a bodiless stranger has stolen inside his body, startling him by doing calisthenics, and he feels himself coming slowly back to life. His body chemistry changes and he is flushed with new strength.

When she first comes to him his heart is empty, a desolate place, a dehydrated oasis, unsolaced, and he's craving womanfood, without which sustenance the tension of his manhood has unwound and relaxed. He has imperative need of the kindness, sympathy, understanding, and conversation of a woman, to hear a woman's laughter at his words, to answer her questions and be answered by her, to look into her eyes, to sniff her primeval fragrance, to hear – with slaughtered ears – the sensuous rustling of frivolous garments as legs are crossed and uncrossed beneath a table, to feel the delicate, shy weight of her hand in his – how painfully and totally aware is he of her presence, her every movement! It is as if one had been left to die beneath a bush on a lonely trail. The sun is hot and the shade of the bush, if not offering an extension of life, offers at least a slowing-down of death. And just when one feels the next breath will surely be the last, a rare and rainbow-colored bird settles on a delicate twig of the bush and, with the magic of melodious trillings and beauty of plumage, charms the dying one back to life. The dying man feels the strength flowing into and through the conduits of his body from the charged atmosphere created by the presence of the bird, and he knows intuitively in his clinging to life that if the bird remains he will regain his strength and health – and live.

Seeing her image slipping away from the weak fingers of his mind as soon as she has gone, his mind fights for a token of her on which to peg memory. Jealously, he hoards the fading memory of their encounter, like a miser gloating over a folio of blue-chip stock. The unfathomable machinery of the subconscious projects an image on to the conscious mind : her bare right arm, from curve of shoulder to finger-tip. (Had his lips quivered with desire to brand that soft, cool-looking flesh with a kiss of fire, had his fingers itched to caress?) Such is the magic of a woman, the female principle of nature which she embodies, and her power to resurrect and revitalize a long-isolated and lonely man.

I was eighteen when I came to prison and of course I have changed tremendously over the years. But I had always had a strong sense of myself and in the last few years I felt I was losing my identity. There was a deadness in my body that eluded me, as though I could not exactly locate its site. I would be aware of this numbness, this feeling of atrophy, and it haunted the back of my mind. Because of this numb spot, I felt peculiarly off balance, the awareness of something missing, of a blank spot, a certain intimation of emptiness. Now I know what it was. After eight years in prison, I was visited by a woman, a woman who was interested in my work and cared about what happened to me. And since encountering her, I feel life, strength flowing back into that spot. My step, the tread of my stride, which was becoming tentative and uncertain, has begun to recover a definiteness, a confidence, a boldness which makes me want to kick over a few tables. I may even swagger a little, and, as I read in a book somewhere, 'push myself forward like a train'.

INITIAL REACTIONS ON THE ASSASSINATION OF MALCOLM X

Folsom Prison,
June 19th, 1965

Sunday is Movie Day at Folsom Prison and I was sitting in the darkened hulk of Mess Hall No. 1 – which convicts call 'The Folsom Theatre' – watching Victor Buono in a movie called *The Strangler*, when a convict known as Silly Willie came over to where I was sitting and whispered into my ear:

'Brother J sent me in to tell you it just came over the TV that Malcolm X was shot as he addressed a rally in New York.'

For a moment the earth seemed to reel in orbit. The skin all over my body tightened up. 'How bad?' I asked.

'The TV didn't say,' answered Silly Willie. The distress was obvious in his voice. 'We was around back in Pipe Alley checking TV when a special bulletin came on. All they said was Malcolm X was shot and they were rushing him to the hospital.'

'Thanks,' I said to Silly Willie. I felt his reassuring hand on my shoulder as he faded away in the darkness. For a moment I pondered whether to go outside and get more information, but something made me hang back. I remember distinctly thinking that I would know soon enough. On the screen before me, Victor Buono had a woman by the throat and was frantically choking the last gasping twitches of life out of her slumping body. I was thinking that if Malcolm's wounds were not too serious, that if he recovered, the shooting might prove to be a blessing in disguise : it would focus more intensified attention on him and create a windfall of sympathy and support for him throughout America's black ghettos, and so put more power into his hands. The possibility that the wounds may have been fatal, that as I sat there Malcolm was lying already dead, was excluded from my mind.

After the movie ended, as I filed outside in the long line of convicts and saw the shocked, wild expression on Brother J's face, I still could not believe that Malcolm X was dead. We mingled in the crowd of convicts milling around in the yard and were immediately surrounded by a group of Muslims, all of whom, like myself, were firm supporters of Malcolm X. He's dead, their faces said, although not one of them spoke a word. As we stood there in silence, two Negro inmates walked by and one of them said to us, 'That's a goddam shame how they killed that man ! Of all people, why'd they kill Malcolm ? Why'n't they kill some of them Uncle-Tomming m.f.'s ? I wish I could get my hands on whoever did it.' And he walked away, talking and cursing to his buddy.

What does one say to his comrades at the moment when The Leader falls ? All comment seems irrelevant. If the source of death is so-called natural causes, or an accident, the reaction is predictable, a feeling of impotence, humbleness, helplessness before the forces of the universe. But when the cause of death is an assassin's bullet, the overpowering desire is for vengeance. One wants to strike out, to kill, crush, destroy, to deliver a telling counterblow, to inflict upon the enemy a reciprocal, equivalent loss. But whom does one strike down at such a time if one happens to be in an anonymous, amorphous crowd of convicts in Folsom Prison and The Leader lies dead thousands of miles away across the continent?

'I'm going to my cell,' I told the tight little knot of Muslims. 'Allah is the Best Knower. Everything will be made manifest in time. Give it a little time. *As-Salaam Aliakum*.'

'*Wa-Aliakum Salaam*,' the Brothers returned the salutation and we shook hands all around, the double handshake which is very popular among Muslims in California prisons. (It is so popular that one sometimes grows weary of shaking hands. If a Muslim leaves a group for a minute to go get a drink of water, he is not unlikely to shake hands all around before he leaves and again when he returns. But no one complains and the convention is respected as a gesture of unity, brotherly love, and solidarity – so meaningful in a situation where Muslims are persecuted and denied recognition and the right to function as a legitimate religion.) I headed for my cell. I lived in No. 5 Building, which is Folsom's Honor Unit, reserved for those who have maintained a clean record for at least six months. Advantages: a larger cell, TV every Wednesday, Saturday, and Sunday night, less custodial supervision, easier ingress and egress. If while living in the Honor Unit you get into a 'beef' which results in action against you by the disciplinary committee, one of the certain penalties is that you are immediately kicked out of No. 5 Building.

As I walked along the first tier toward my cell, I ran into Red, who lived near me on the tier.

'I guess you heard about Malcolm?'

'Yeah,' I said. 'They say he got wasted.'

Red, who is white, knew from our many discussions that I was extremely partial to Malcolm, and he himself, being thoroughly alienated from the *status quo*, recognized the assassination for what it was: a negative blow against a positive force. Red's questions were the obvious ones: Who? Why? The questions were advanced tentatively, cautiously, because of the treacherous ground he was on: a redheaded, blue-eyed white man concerned by an event which so many others greeted with smiles and sighs. I went into my cell.

Although I heard it blared over the radio constantly and read about it in all the newspapers, days passed during which my mind continued to reject the fact of Malcolm's death. I existed in a dazed state, wandering in a trance around Folsom, drifting through the working hours in the prison bakery; and yet I was keen to observe the effect of the assassination on my fellow inmates. From most of the whites there was a leer and a hint of a smile in the eyes. They seemed anxious to see a war break out between the followers of Elijah and the followers of Malcolm.

There are only a few whites in Folsom with whom I would ever discuss the death of Malcolm or anything else besides baseball or the weather. Many of the Mexican-Americans were sympathetic, although some of them made a point, when being observed by whites, of letting drop sly remarks indicating they were glad Malcolm was gone. Among the Negroes there was mass mourning for Malcolm X. Nobody talked much for a few days. The only Negroes who were not indignant were a few of the Muslims who remained loyal to Elijah Muhammad. They interpreted Malcolm's assassination as the will of Allah descending upon his head for having gone astray. To them, it was Divine chastisement and a warning to those whom Malcolm had tempted. It was not so much Malcolm's death that made them glad; but in their eyes it now seemed possible to heal the schism in the movement and restore the monolithic unity of the Nation of Islam, a unity they looked back on with some nostalgia.

Many Negro convicts saw Malcolm's assassination as a historic turning point in black America. Whereas Negroes often talk heatedly about wiping out all the so-called Negro leaders whom they do not happen to like or agree with, this was the first significant case of Negro leader-killing that anyone could remember. What struck me is that the Negro convicts welcomed the new era. If a man as valuable to us as Malcolm could go down, then as far as I was concerned so could any other man – myself included. Coming a week after the alleged exposé of the alleged plot to dynamite the Statue of Liberty, Washington Monument, and the Liberty Bell, a plot supposedly hatched by discontented blacks, the assassination of Malcolm X had put new ideas in the wind with implications for the future of black struggle in America.

I suppose that like many of the brothers and sisters in the Nation of Islam movement, I also had clung to the hope that, somehow, the rift between Malcolm X and Elijah Muhammad would be mended. As long as Brother Malcolm was alive, many Muslims could maintain this hope, neatly overlooking the increasing bitterness of their rivalry. But death made the split final and sealed it for history. These events caused a profound personal crisis in my life and beliefs, as it did for other Muslims. During the bitter time of his suspension and prior to his break with Elijah Muhammad, we had watched Malcolm X as he sought frantically to reorient himself and establish a new platform. It was like watching a master do a dance with death on a highstrung tightrope. He pirouetted, twirled, turned somersaults in the air – but he landed firmly on his feet and was off and running. We watched it all, seeking a cause to condemn Malcolm X and cast him out of our hearts. We read all the charges and countercharges. I found Malcolm X blameless.

It had been my experience that the quickest way to become hated by the Muslims was to criticize Elijah Muhammad or disagree with something he wrote or said. If Elijah wrote, as he has done, that the swine is a poison creature composed of a third rat, a third cat, and a third dog and you attempted to cite scientific facts to challenge this, you had sinned against the light, that was all there was to it. How much more unlikely was it, therefore, that Muslims would stand up and denounce Elijah himself, repudiate his authority and his theology, deny his revelation, and take sides against him, the Messenger of Almighty God Allah? I never dreamed that someday I would be cast in that hapless role.

After Malcolm made his pilgrimage to Mecca, completing a triumphal tour of Africa and the Near East, during which he received the high honors of a visiting dignitary, he returned to the U.S.A. and set about building his newly founded Organization of Afro-American Unity. He also established the Muslim Mosque, Inc., to receive the Muslims he thought would pull away from Elijah. The Muslim Mosque would teach Orthodox Islam, under the direction of Sheikh Ahmed Hassoun from the Holy City of Mecca. Grand Sheikh Muhammad Sarur Al-Sabban, secretary-general of the Muslim World League, had offered the services of Sheikh Ahmed, according to the Los Angeles *Herald-Dispatch*, to 'help Malcolm X in his efforts to correct the distorted image that the religion of Islam has been given by hate groups in this country'.

I began defending Malcolm X. At a secret meeting of the Muslims in Folsom, I announced that I was no longer a follower of Elijah Muhammad, that I was throwing my support behind Brother Malcolm. I urged everyone there to think the matter over and make a choice, because it was no longer possible to ride two horses at the same time. On the wall of my cell I had a large, framed picture of Elijah Muhammad which I had had for years. I took it down, destroyed it, and in its place put up, in the same frame, a beautiful picture of Malcolm X kneeling down in the Mohammed Ali Mosque in Cairo, which I clipped from the *Saturday Evening Post*. At first the other Muslims in Folsom denounced me; some I'd known intimately for years stopped speaking to me or even looking at me. When we met, they averted their eyes. To them the choice was simple: Elijah Muhammad is the hand-picked Messenger of Allah, the instrument of Allah's Will. All who oppose him are aiding Allah's enemies, the White Devils. Whom do you choose, God or the Devil? Malcolm X, in the eyes of Elijah's followers, had committed the unforgivable heresy when, changing his views and abandoning the racist position, he admitted the possibility of brotherhood between blacks and whites. In a letter sent back to the U.S. from the Holy Land, Malcolm X had stated:

You may be shocked by these words coming from me, but I have always been a man who tries to face facts and to accept the reality of life as

43

new experiences and knowledge unfold it. The experiences of this pilgrimage have taught me much and each hour in the Holy Land opens my eyes even more ... I have eaten from the same plate with people whose eyes were the bluest of blue, whose hair was the blondest of blond and whose skin was the whitest of white ... and I felt the sincerity in the words and deeds of these 'white' Muslims that I felt among the African Muslims of Nigeria, Sudan and Ghana.

Many of us were shocked and outraged by these words from Malcolm X, who had been a major influence upon us all and the main factor in many of our conversions to the Black Muslims. But there were those of us who were glad to be liberated from a doctrine of hate and racial supremacy. The onus of teaching racial supremacy and hate, which is the white man's burden, is pretty hard to bear. Asked if he would accept whites as members of his Organization of Afro-American Unity, Malcolm said he would accept John Brown if he were around today – which certainly is setting the standard high.

At the moment I declared myself for Malcolm X, I had some prestige among the Muslims in the prisons of California, because of my active role in proselytizing new converts and campaigning for religious freedom for Muslim convicts. We sent a barrage of letters and petitions to the courts, governmental officials, even the United Nations.

After the death of Brother Booker T. X., who was shot dead by a San Quentin prison guard, and who at the time had been my cell partner and the inmate Minister of the Muslims of San Quentin, my leadership of the Muslims of San Quentin had been publicly endorsed by Elijah Muhammad's west coast representative, Minister John Shabazz of Muhammad's Los Angeles Mosque. This was done because of the explosive conditions in San Quentin at the time. Muslim officials wanted to avert any Muslim-initiated violence, which had become a distinct possibility in the aftermath of Brother Booker's death. I was instructed to impose an iron discipline upon the San Quentin Mosque, which had continued to exist despite the unending efforts of prison authorities to stamp it out. Most of the Muslims who were in prison during those days have since been released. I was one of the few remaining, and I was therefore looked upon by the other Muslims as one who had sacrificed and invested much in the struggle to advance the teachings of Elijah Muhammad. For that reason, my defection to Malcolm X caused a great deal of consternation among the Muslims of Folsom. But slowly, Malcolm was getting his machine together and it was obvious to me that his influence was growing. Negro inmates who had had reservations about Malcolm while he was under Elijah's authority now embraced him, and it was clear that they accepted Malcolm's leadership. Negroes whom we had tried in vain for years to convert to Elijah's fold now lined up with enthusiasm behind Malcolm.

I ran a regular public relations campaign for Malcolm in Folsom. I saw to it that copies of his speeches were made and circulated among Negro inmates. I never missed a chance to speak favorably about Malcolm, to quote him, to explain and justify what he was trying to do. Soon I had the ear of the Muslims, and it was not long before Malcolm had other ardent defenders in Folsom. In a very short time Malcolm became the hero of the vast majority of Negro inmates. Elijah Muhammad was quickly becoming irrelevant, passé.

Malcolm X had a special meaning for black convicts. A former prisoner himself, he had risen from the lowest depths to great heights. For this reason he was a symbol of hope, a model for thousands of black convicts who found themselves trapped in the vicious P.P.P. cycle: prison-parole-prison. One thing that the judges, policemen, and administrators of prisons seem never to have understood, and for which they certainly do not make any allowances, is that Negro convicts, basically, rather than see themselves as criminals and perpetrators of misdeeds, look upon themselves as prisoners-of-war, the victims of a vicious, dog-eat-dog social system that is so heinous as to cancel out their own malefactions: in the jungle there is no right or wrong.

Rather than owing and paying a debt to society, Negro prisoners feel that they are being abused, that their imprisonment is simply another form of the oppression which they have known all their lives. Negro inmates feel that they are being robbed, that it is 'society' that owes them, that should be paying them, a debt.

America's penology does not take this into account. Malcolm X did, and black convicts know that the ascension to power of Malcolm X or a man like him would eventually have revolutionized penology in America. Malcolm delivered a merciless and damning indictment of prevailing penology. It is only a matter of time until the question of the prisoner's debt to society versus society's debt to the prisoner is injected forcefully into national and state politics, into the civil and human rights struggle, and into the consciousness of the body politic. It is an explosive issue which goes to the very root of America's system of justice, the structure of criminal law, the prevailing beliefs and attitudes toward the convicted felon. While it is easier to make out a case for black convicts, the same principles apply to white and Mexican-American convicts as well. They too are victimized, albeit a little more subtly, by 'society'. When black convicts start demanding a new dispensation and definition of justice, naturally the white and Mexican-American convicts will demand equality of treatment. Malcolm X was a focus for these aspirations.

The Black Muslim movement was destroyed the moment Elijah cracked the whip over Malcolm's head, because it was not the Black Muslim movement itself that was so irresistibly appealing to the true believers. It was the awakening into self-consciousness of twenty million Negroes which was so compelling. Malcolm X articulated their aspirations better than any other man of our time. When he spoke under the banner of Elijah Muhammad he was irresistible. When he spoke under his own banner he was still irresistible. If he had become a Quaker, a Catholic, or a Seventh-Day Adventist, or a Sammy Davis-style Jew, and if he had continued to give voice to the mute ambitions in the black man's soul, his message would still have been triumphant: because what was great was not Malcolm X but the truth he uttered.

The truth which Malcolm uttered had vanquished the whole passle of so-called Negro leaders and spokesmen who trifle and compromise with the truth in order to curry favor with the white power structure. He was stopped in the only way such a man can be stopped, in the same way that the enemies of the

Congolese people had to stop Lumumba, by the same method that exploiters, tyrants, and parasitical oppressors have always crushed the legitimate strivings of people for freedom, justice, and equality – by murder, assassination, and mad-dog butchery.

What provoked the assassins to murder? Did it bother them that Malcolm was elevating our struggle into the international arena through his campaign to carry it before the United Nations? Well, by murdering him they only hastened the process, because we certainly are going to take our cause before a sympathetic world. Did it bother the assassins that Malcolm denounced the racist strait-jacket demonology of Elijah Muhammad? Well, we certainly do denounce it and will continue to do so. Did it bother the assassins that Malcolm taught us to defend ourselves? We shall not remain a defenseless prey to the murderer, to the sniper and the bomber. In so far as Malcolm spoke the truth, the truth will triumph and prevail and his name shall live; and in so far as those who opposed him lied, to that extent will their names become curses. Because 'truth crushed to earth shall rise again'.

So now Malcolm is no more. The bootlickers, Uncle Toms, lackeys, and stooges of the white power structure have done their best to denigrate Malcolm, to root him out of his people's heart, to tarnish his memory. But their million-worded lies fall on deaf ears. As Ossie Davis so eloquently expressed it in his immortal eulogy of Malcolm:

If you knew him you would know why we must honor him: Malcolm was our manhood, our living, black manhood! This was his meaning to his people. And, in honoring him, we honor the best in ourselves ... However much we may have differed with him – or with each other about him and his value as a man – let his going from us serve only to bring us together, now. Consigning these mortal remains to earth, the common mother of all, secure in the knowledge that what we place in the ground is no more now a man – but a seed – which, after the winter of our discontent, will come forth again to meet us. And we will know him then for what he was and is – a Prince – our own black shining Prince! – who didn't hesitate to die, because he loved us so.

We shall have our manhood. We shall have it or the earth will be leveled by our attempts to gain it.

Part Two

BLOOD OF THE BEAST

THE WHITE RACE AND ITS
HEROES

White people cannot, in the generality, be taken as models of
how to live. Rather, the white man is himself in sore need of
new standards, which will release him from his confusion and
place him once again in fruitful communion with the depths
of his own being.

James Baldwin: *The Fire Next Time*

Right from the go, let me make one thing absolutely
clear: I am not now, nor have I ever been, a white
man. Nor, I hasten to add, am I now a Black Muslim
– although I used to be. But I *am* an Ofay Watcher,
a member of that unchartered, amorphous league
which has members on all continents and the
islands of the seas. Ofay Watchers Anonymous,
we might be called, because we exist concealed in
the shadows wherever colored people have known
oppression by whites, by white enslavers, colonizers,
imperialists, and neo-colonialists.

Did it irritate you, compatriot, for me to string
those epithets out like that? Tolerate me. My intention was not necessarily to sprinkle salt over anyone's
wounds. I did it primarily to relieve a certain pressure
on my brain. Do you cop that? If not, then we're in
trouble, because we Ofay Watchers have a pro-
nounced tendency to slip into that mood. If it is
bothersome to you, it is quite a task for me because
not too long ago it was my way of life to preach,

53

as ardently as I could, that the white race is a race of devils, created by their maker to do evil, and make evil appear as good; that the white race is the natural, unchangeable enemy of the black man, who is the original man, owner, maker, cream of the planet Earth; that the white race was soon to be destroyed by Allah, and that the black man would then inherit the earth, which has always, in fact, been his.

I have, so to speak, washed my hands in the blood of the martyr, Malcolm X, whose retreat from the precipice of madness created new room for others to turn about in, and I am now caught up in that tiny space, attempting a maneuver of my own. Having renounced the teachings of Elijah Muhammad, I find that a rebirth does not follow automatically, of its own accord, that a void is left in one's vision, and this void seeks constantly to obliterate itself by pulling one back to one's former outlook. I have tried a tentative compromise by adopting a select vocabulary, so that now when I see the whites of *their* eyes, instead of saying 'devil' or 'beast' I say 'imperialist' or 'colonialist', and everyone seems to be happier.

In silence, we have spent our years watching the ofays, trying to understand them, on the principle that you have a better chance of coping with the known than with the unknown. Some of us have been, and some still are, interested in learning whether it is *ultimately* possible to live in the same territory with people who seem so disagreeable to live with; still others want to get as far away from ofays as possible. What we share in common is the desire to break the ofays' power over us.

At times of fundamental social change, such as the era in which we live, it is easy to be deceived by the onrush of events, beguiled by the craving for social stability into mistaking transitory phenomena for enduring reality. The strength and permanence of 'white backlash' in America is just such an illusion. However much this rear-guard action might seem to grow in strength, the initiative, and the future, rest with those whites and blacks who have liberated themselves from the master/slave syndrome. And these are to be found mainly among the youth.

Over the past twelve years there has surfaced a political conflict between the generations that is deeper, even, than the struggle between the races. Its first dramatic manifestation was within the ranks of the Negro people, when college students in the South, fed up with Uncle Tom's hat-in-hand approach to revolution, threw off the yoke of the N.A.A.C.P. When these students initiated the first sit-ins, their spirit spread like a raging fire across the nation, and the technique of non-violent direct action, constantly refined and honed into a sharp cutting tool, swiftly matured. The older Negro 'leaders', who are now all die-hard advocates of this tactic, scolded the students for sitting-in. The students rained down contempt upon their hoary heads. In the pre-sit-in days, these conservative leaders had always succeeded in putting down insurgent elements among the Negro people. (A measure of their power, prior to the students' rebellion, is shown by their success in isolating such great black men as the late W. E. B. DuBois and Paul Robeson, when these stalwarts, refusing to bite their tongues, lost favor with the U.S. government by their unstinting efforts to link up the Negro revolution with national liberation movements around the world.)

The 'Negro leaders', and the whites who depended upon them to control their people, were outraged by the impudence of the students. Calling for a moratorium on student initiative, they were greeted instead by an encore of sit-ins, and retired to their ivory towers to contemplate the new phenomenon. Others, less prudent because held on a tighter leash by the whites, had their careers brought to an abrupt end because they thought they could lead a black/white backlash against the students, only to find themselves in a kind of Bay of Pigs. Negro college presidents, who expelled students from all-Negro colleges in an attempt to quash the demonstrations, ended up losing their jobs; the victorious students would no longer allow them to preside over the campuses. The spontaneous protests on southern campuses over the repressive measures of their college administrations were an earnest of the Free Speech upheaval which years later was to shake the U.C. campus at Berkeley. In countless ways, the rebellion of the black students served as catalyst for the brewing revolt of the whites.

What has suddenly happened is that the white race has lost its heroes. Worse, its heroes have been revealed as villains and its greatest heroes as the arch-villains. The new generations of whites, appalled by the sanguine and despicable record carved over the face of the globe by their race in the last five hundred years, are rejecting the panoply of white heroes, whose heroism consisted in erecting the inglorious edifice of colonialism and imperialism; heroes whose careers rested on a system of foreign and domestic exploitation, rooted in the myth of white supremacy and the manifest destiny of the white race. The emerging shape of a new world order, and the requisites for survival in such a world, are fostering in young whites a new outlook. They recoil in

shame from the spectacle of cowboys and pioneers –
their heroic forefathers whose exploits filled earlier
generations with pride – galloping across a movie
screen shooting down Indians like Coke bottles. Even
Winston Churchill, who is looked upon by older
whites as perhaps the greatest hero of the twentieth
century – even he, because of the system of which he
was a creature and which he served, is an arch-villain
in the eyes of the young white rebels.

At the close of World War Two, national liberation
movements in the colonized world picked up new
momentum and audacity, seeking to cash in on the
democratic promises made by the Allies during the
war. The Atlantic Charter, signed by President Roose-
velt and Prime Minister Churchill in 1941, affirming
'the right of all people to choose the form of government under which they may live', established the
principle, although it took years of postwar struggle
to give this piece of rhetoric even the appearance of
reality. And just as world revolution has prompted
the oppressed to re-evaluate their self-image in terms
of the changing conditions, to slough off the servile
attitudes inculcated by long years of subordination,
the same dynamics of change have prompted the
white people of the world to re-evaluate their self-
image as well, to disabuse themselves of the Master
Race psychology developed over centuries of imperial
hegemony.

It is among the white youth of the world that the
greatest change is taking place. It is they who are
experiencing the great psychic pain of waking into
consciousness to find their inherited heroes turned
by events into villains. Communication and understanding between the older and younger generations
of whites has entered a crisis. The elders, who, in the

tradition of privileged classes or races, genuinely do not understand the youth, trapped by old ways of thinking and blind to the future, have only just begun to be vexed – because the youth have only just begun to rebel. So thoroughgoing is the revolution in the psyches of white youth that the traditional tolerance which every older generation has found it necessary to display is quickly exhausted, leaving a gulf of fear, hostility, mutual misunderstanding, and contempt.

The rebellion of the oppressed peoples of the world, along with the Negro revolution in America, have opened the way to a new evaluation of history, a re-examination of the role played by the white race since the beginning of European expansion. The positive achievements are also there in the record, and future generations will applaud them. But there can be no applause now, not while the master still holds the whip in his hand! Not even the master's own children can find it possible to applaud him – he cannot even applaud himself! The negative rings too loudly. Slave-catchers, slave-owners, murderers, butchers, invaders, oppressors – the white heroes have acquired new names. The great white statesmen whom school children are taught to revere are revealed as the architects of systems of human exploitation and slavery. Religious leaders are exposed as condoners and justifiers of all these evil deeds. School teachers and college professors are seen as a clique of brainwashers and whitewashers.

The white youth of today are coming to see, intuitively, that to escape the onus of the history their fathers made they must face and admit the moral truth concerning the works of their fathers. That such venerated figures as George Washington and Thomas Jefferson owned hundreds of black slaves, that all of the Presidents up to Lincoln presided over a slave state, and that every President since Lincoln connived politically and cynically with the issues affecting the human rights and general welfare of the broad masses of the American people – these facts weigh heavily upon the hearts of these young people.

The elders do not like to give these youngsters credit for being able to understand what is going on and what has gone on. When speaking of juvenile delinquency, or the rebellious attitude of today's youth, the elders employ a glib rhetoric. They speak of the 'alienation of youth', the desire of the young to be independent, the problems of 'the father image' and 'the mother image' and their effect upon growing children who lack sound models upon which to pattern themselves. But they consider it bad form to connect the problems of the youth with the central event of our era – the national liberation movements abroad and the Negro revolution at home. The foundations of authority have been blasted to bits in America because the whole society has been indicted, tried, and convicted of injustice. To the youth, the elders are Ugly Americans; to the elders, the youth have gone mad.

The rebellion of the white youth has gone through four broadly discernible stages. First there was an initial recoiling away, a rejection of the conformity which America expected, and had always received, sooner or later, from its youth. The disaffected youth were refusing to participate in the system, having discovered that America, far from helping the underdog, was up to its ears in the mud trying to hold the dog down. Because of the publicity and self-advertisements of the more vocal rebels, this period has come to be

59

known as the beatnik era, although not all of the youth affected by these changes thought of themselves as beatniks. The howl of the beatniks and their scathing, outraged denunciation of the system – characterized by Ginsberg as Moloch, a bloodthirsty Semitic deity to which the ancient tribes sacrificed their firstborn children – was a serious, irrevocable declaration of war. It is revealing that the elders looked upon the beatniks as mere obscene misfits who were too lazy to take baths and too stingy to buy a haircut. The elders had eyes but couldn't see, ears but couldn't hear – not even when the message came through as clearly as in this remarkable passage from Jack Kerouac's *On the Road*:

> At lilac evening I walked with every muscle aching among the lights of 27th and Welton in the Denver colored section, wishing I were a Negro, feeling that the best the white world had offered was not enough ecstasy for me, not enough life, joy, kicks, darkness, music, not enough night. I wished I were a Denver Mexican, or even a poor overworked Jap, anything but what I so drearily was, a 'white man' disillusioned. All my life I'd had white ambitions ... I passed the dark porches of Mexican and Negro homes; soft voices were there, occasionally the dusky knee of some mysterious sensuous gal; the dark faces of the men behind rose arbors. Little children sat like sages in ancient rocking chairs.

The second stage arrived when these young people, having decided emphatically that the world, and particularly the U.S.A., was unacceptable to them in its present form, began an active search for roles they could play in changing society. If many of these young people were content to lay up in their cool beat pads, smoking pot and listening to jazz in a perpetual orgy of esoteric bliss, there were others, less crushed by the system, who recognized the need for positive action. Moloch could not ask for anything more than to have its disaffected victims withdraw into safe, passive, apolitical little nonparticipatory islands, in an economy less and less able to provide jobs for the growing pool of unemployed. If all the unemployed had followed the lead of the beatniks, Moloch would gladly have legalized the use of euphoric drugs and marijuana, passed out free jazz albums and sleeping bags, to all those willing to sign affidavits promising to remain 'beat'. The non-beat disenchanted white youth were attracted magnetically to the Negro revolution, which had begun to take on a mass, insurrectionary tone. But they had difficulty understanding their relationship to the Negro, and what role 'whites' could play in a 'Negro revolution'. For the time being they watched the Negro activists from afar.

The third stage, which is rapidly drawing to a close, emerged when white youth started joining Negro demonstrations in large numbers. The presence of whites among the demonstrators emboldened the Negro leaders and allowed them to use tactics they never would have been able to employ with all-black troops. The racist conscience of America is such that murder does not register as murder, really, unless the victim is white. And it was only when the newspapers and magazines started carrying pictures and stories of white demonstrators being beaten and maimed by mobs and police that the public began to protest. Negroes have become so used to this double standard that they, too, react differently to the death of a white. When white freedom riders were brutalized along with blacks, a sigh of relief went up from the black masses, because the blacks knew that white blood is the coin of freedom in a land where for four hundred years black blood has been shed unremarked and with impunity. America has never truly been outraged by the murder of a black man, woman, or child. White politicians may, if Negroes are aroused by a particular murder, say with their lips what they know with their minds they should feel with their hearts – but don't.

It is a measure of what the Negro feels that when the two white and one black civil rights workers were murdered in Mississippi in 1964, the event was welcomed by Negroes on a level of understanding beyond and deeper than the grief they felt for the victims and their families. This welcoming of violence and death to whites can amost be heard – indeed it can be heard – in the inevitable words, oft repeated by Negroes, that those whites, and blacks, do not die in vain. So it was with Mrs Viola Liuzzo. And much of the anger which Negroes felt toward Martin Luther King during the Battle of Selma stemmed from the fact that he denied history a great moment, never to be recaptured, when he turned tail on the Edmund Pettus Bridge and refused to all those whites behind him what they had traveled thousands of miles to receive. If the police had turned them back by force, all those nuns, priests, rabbis, preachers, and distinguished ladies and gentlemen old and young – as they had done the Negroes a week earlier – the violence and brutality of the system would have been ruthlessly exposed. Or if, seeing King determined to lead them on to Montgomery, the troopers had stepped aside to avoid precisely the confrontation that Washington would not have tolerated, it would have signaled the capitulation of the militant white South. As it turned out, the March on Montgomery was a show of somewhat dim luster, stage-managed by the Establishment. But by this time the young whites were already active participants in the Negro revolution. In fact they had begun to transform it into something broader, with the potential of encompassing the whole of America in a radical reordering of society.

The fourth stage, now in its infancy, sees this white youth taking the initiative, using techniques learned in the Negro struggle to attack problems in the general society. The classic example of this new energy in action was the student battle in the U.C. campus at Berkeley, California – the free speech movement. Leading the revolt were veterans of the civil rights movement, some of whom spent time on the firing line in the wilderness of Mississippi/Alabama. Flowing from the same momentum were student demonstrations against U.S. interference in the internal affairs of Vietnam, Cuba, the Dominican Republic, and the Congo and U.S. aid to apartheid in South Africa. The students even aroused the intellectual community to actions and positions unthinkable a few years ago: witness the teach-ins. But their revolt is deeper than single-issue protest. The characteristics of the white rebels which most alarm their elders – the long hair, the new dances, their love for Negro music, their use of marijuana, their mystical attitude toward sex – are all tools of their rebellion. They have turned these tools against the totalitarian fabric of American society – and they mean to change it.

From the beginning, America has been a schizophrenic nation. Its two conflicting images of itself were never reconciled, because never before has the survival of its most cherished myths made a reconciliation mandatory. Once before, during the bitter struggle between North and South climaxed by the Civil War, the two images of America came into conflict, although whites North and South scarcely understood it. The image of America held by its most alienated citizens was advanced neither by the North nor by the South; it was perhaps best expressed by Frederick Douglass, who was born into slavery in 1817, escaped to the North, and became the greatest leader-spokesman for the blacks of his era. In words that can still, years later, arouse an audience of black Americans, Frederick Douglass delivered, in 1852, a scorching indictment in his Fourth of July oration in Rochester:

What to the American slave is your Fourth of July? I answer: a day that reveals to him, more than all other days in the year, the gross injustice and cruelty to which he is the constant victim. To him your celebration is a sham; your boasted liberty, an unholy licence; your national greatness, swelling vanity; your sounds of rejoicing are empty and heartless; your denunciation of tyrants, brass-fronted impudence; your shouts of liberty and equality, hollow mockery; your prayers and hymns, your sermons and thanksgivings, with all your religious parade and solemnity, are, to him, more bombast, fraud, deception, impiety and hypocrisy – a thin veil to cover up crimes which would disgrace a nation of savages ...

You boast of your love of liberty, your superior civilization, and pure Christianity, while the whole political power of the nation (as embodied in the two great political parties) is solemnly pledged to support and perpetuate the enslavement of three millions of your countrymen. You hurl your anathemas at the crown-headed tyrants of Russia and Austria and pride yourselves on your democratic institutions, while you yourselves consent to be the mere *tools* and *bodyguards* of the tyrants of Virginia and Carolina.

You invite to your shores fugitives of oppression from abroad, honor them with banquets, greet them with ovations, cheer them, toast them, salute them, protect them, and pour out your money to them like water; but the fugitive from your own land you advertise, hunt, arrest, shoot, and kill. You glory in your refinement and your universal education; yet you maintain a system as barbarous and dreadful as ever stained the character of a nation – a system begun in avarice, supported in pride, and perpetuated in cruelty.

You shed tears over fallen Hungary, and make the sad story of her wrongs the theme of your poets, statesmen and orators, till your gallant sons are ready to fly to arms to vindicate her cause against the oppressor; but, in regard to the ten thousand wrongs of the American slave, you would enforce the strictest silence, and would hail him as an enemy of the nation who dares to make these wrongs the subject of public discourse!

This most alienated view of America was preached

by the Abolitionists, and by Harriet Beecher Stowe in her *Uncle Tom's Cabin*. But such a view of America was too distasteful to receive wide attention, and serious debate about America's image and her reality was engaged in only on the fringes of society. Even when confronted with overwhelming evidence to the contrary, most white Americans have found it possible, after steadying their rattled nerves, to settle comfortably back into their vaunted belief that America is dedicated to the proposition that all men are created equal and endowed by their Creator with certain inalienable rights – life, liberty and the pursuit of happiness. With the Constitution for a rudder and the Declaration of Independence as its guiding star, the ship of state is sailing always toward a brighter vision of freedom and justice for all.

Because there is no common ground between these two contradictory images of America, they had to be kept apart. But the moment the blacks were let into the white world – let out of the voiceless and faceless cages of their ghettos, singing, walking, talking, dancing, writing, and orating *their* image of America and of Americans – the white world was suddenly challenged to match its practice to its preachments. And this is why those whites who abandon the *white* image of America and adopt the *black* are greeted with such unmitigated hostility by their elders.

For all these years whites have been taught to believe in the myth they preached, while Negroes have had to face the bitter reality of what America practiced. But without the lies and distortions, white Americans would not have been able to do the things they have done. When whites are forced to look honestly upon the objective proof of their deeds, the cement of mendacity holding white society together swiftly disintegrates. On the other hand, the core of the black world's vision remains intact, and in fact begins to expand and spread into the psychological territory vacated by the non-viable white lies, i.e., into the minds of young whites. It is remarkable how the system worked for so many years, how the majority of whites remained effectively unaware of any contradiction between their view of the world and that world itself. The mechanism by which this was rendered possible requires examination at this point.

Let us recall that the white man, in order to justify slavery and, later on, to justify segregation, elaborated a complex, all-pervasive myth which at one time classified the black man as a subhuman beast of burden. The myth was progressively modified, gradually elevating the blacks on the scale of evolution, following their slowly changing status, until the plateau of separate-but-equal was reached at the close of the nineteenth century. During slavery, the black was seen as a mindless Supermasculine Menial. Forced to do the backbreaking work, he was conceived in terms of his ability to do such work – 'field niggers', etc. The white man administered the plantation, doing all the thinking, exercising omnipotent power over the slaves. He had little difficulty dissociating himself from the black slaves, and he could not conceive of their positions being reversed or even reversible.

Blacks and whites being conceived as mutually exclusive types, those attributes imputed to the blacks could not also be imputed to the whites – at least not in equal degree – without blurring the line separating the races. These images were based upon the social function of the two races, the work they performed. The ideal white man was one who knew how to use his head, who knew how to manage and control things and get things done. Those whites who were not in a position to perform these functions nevertheless aspired to them. The ideal black man was one who did exactly as he was told, and did it efficiently and cheerfully. 'Slaves', said Frederick Douglass, 'are generally expected to sing as well as to work.' As the black man's position and function became more varied, the images of white and black, having become stereotypes, lagged behind.

The separate-but-equal doctrine was promulgated by the Supreme Court in 1896. It had the same purpose domestically as the Open Door Policy toward China in the international arena : to stabilize a situation and subordinate a non-white population so that racist exploiters could manipulate those people according to their own selfish interests. These doctrines were foisted off as *the epitome of enlightened justice, the highest expression of morality*. Sanctified by religion, justified by philosophy and legalized by the Supreme Court, separate-but-equal was enforced by day by agencies of the law, and by the K.K.K. & Co. under cover of night. Booker T. Washington, the Martin Luther King of his day, accepted separate-but-equal in the name of all Negroes. W. E. B. DuBois denounced it.

Separate-but-equal marked the last stage of the white man's flight into cultural neurosis, and the beginning of the black man's frantic striving to assert his humanity and equalize his position with the white. Blacks ventured into all fields of endeavor to which they could gain entrance. Their goal was to present in all fields a performance that would equal or surpass that of the whites. It was long axiomatic among blacks that a black had to be twice as competent as a white in any field in order to win grudging recognition from the whites. This produced a pathological motivation in the blacks to equal or surpass the whites, and a pathological motivation in the whites to maintain a distance from the blacks. This is the rack on which black and white Americans receive their delicious torture! At first there was the color bar, flatly denying the blacks entrance to certain spheres of activity. When this no longer worked, and blacks invaded sector after sector of American life and economy, the whites evolved other methods of keeping their distance. The illusion of the Negro's inferior nature had to be maintained.

One device evolved by the whites was to tab whatever the blacks did with the prefix 'Negro'. We had *Negro* literature, *Negro* athletes, *Negro* music, *Negro* doctors, *Negro* politicians, *Negro* workers. The malignant ingeniousness of this device is that although it accurately describes an objective biological fact – or, at least, a sociological fact in America – it concealed the paramount psychological fact: that to the white mind, prefixing anything with 'Negro' automatically consigned it to an inferior category. A well-known example of the white necessity to deny due credit to blacks is in the realm of music. White musicians were famous for going to Harlem and other Negro cultural centers literally to steal the black man's music, carrying it back across the color line into the Great White World and passing off the watered-down loot as their own original creations. Blacks, meanwhile, were ridiculed as *Negro* musicians playing inferior coon music.

The Negro revolution at home and national liberation movements abroad have unceremoniously shattered the world of fantasy in which the whites have
been living. It is painful that many do not yet see
that their fantasy world has been rendered uninhabit-
able in the last half of the twentieth century. But it
is away from this world that the white youth of today
are turning. The 'paper tiger' hero, James Bond, offering the whites a triumphant image of themselves, is
saying what many whites want desperately to hear
reaffirmed: *I am still the White Man, lord of the land,
licensed to kill, and the world is still an empire at my
feet.* James Bond feeds on that secret little anxiety,
the psychological white backlash, felt in some degree
by most whites alive. It is exasperating to see little
brown men and little yellow men from the mysterious
Orient, and the opaque black men of Africa (to say
nothing of these impudent American Negroes!) who
come to the U.N. and talk smart to us, who are scurrying all over *our* globe in their strange modes of dress
– much as if they were new, unpleasant arrivals from
another planet. Many whites believe in their ulcers
that it is only a matter of time before the Marines
get the signal to round up these truants and put them
back securely in their cages. But it is away from this
fantasy world that the white youth of today are
turning.

In the world revolution now under way, the initiative rests with people of color. That growing numbers
of white youth are repudiating their heritage of blood
and taking people of color as their heroes and models
is a tribute not only to their insight but to the resili-
ence of the human spirit. For today the heroes of the
initiative are people not usually thought of as white:
Fidel Castro, Che Guevara, Kwame Nkrumah, Mao

Tse-tung, Gmal Abdel Nasser, Robert F. Williams, Malcolm X, Ben Bella, John Lewis, Martin Luther King, Jr, Robert Parris Moses, Ho Chi Minh, Stokeley Carmichael, W. E. B. DuBois, James Forman, Chou En-lai.

The white youth of today have begun to react to the fact that the 'American Way of Life' is a fossil of history. What do they care if their old baldheaded and crew-cut elders don't dig their caveman mops? They couldn't care less about the old, stiffassed honkies who don't like their new dances: Frug, Monkey, Jerk, Swim, Watusi. All they know is that it feels good to swing to way-out body-rhythms instead of dragassing across the dance floor like zombies to the dead beat of mind-smothered Mickey Mouse music. Is it any wonder that the youth have lost all respect for their elders, for law and order, when for as long as they can remember all they've witnessed is a monumental bickering over the Negro's place in American society and the right of people around the world to be left alone by outside powers? They have witnessed the law, both domestic and international, being spat upon by those who do not like its terms. Is it any wonder, then, that they feel justified, by sitting-in and freedom riding, in breaking laws made by lawless men? Old funny-styled, zipper-mouthed political night riders know nothing but to haul out an investigating committee *to look into the disturbance* to find the cause of the unrest among the youth. Look into a mirror! The cause is you, Mr and Mrs Yesterday, you with your forked tongues.

A young white today cannot help but recoil from the base deeds of his people. On every side, on every continent, he sees racial arrogance, savage brutality

71

toward the conquered and subjugated people, geno-
cide; he sees the human cargo of the slave trade; he
sees the systematic extermination of American
Indians; he sees the civilized nations of Europe fighting in imperial depravity over the lands of other
people – and over possession of the very people themselves. There seems to be no end to the ghastly deeds
of which his people are guilty. GUILTY. The slaughter
of the Jews by the Germans, the dropping of atomic
bombs on the Japanese people – these deeds weigh
heavily upon the prostrate souls and tumultuous con-
sciences of the white youth. The white heroes, their
hands dripping with blood, are dead.

The young whites know that the colored people of
the world, Afro-Americans included, do not seek
revenge for their suffering. They seek the same things
the white rebel wants: an end to war and exploitation. Black and white, the young rebels are free
people, free in a way that Americans have never been
before in the history of their country. And they are
outraged.

There is in America today a generation of white
youth that is truly worthy of a black man's respect,
and this is a rare event in the foul annals of American
history. From the beginning of the contact between
blacks and whites, there has been very little reason
for a black man to respect a white, with such excep-
tions as John Brown and others lesser known. But
respect commands itself and it can neither be given
nor withheld when it is due. If a man like Malcolm
X could change and repudiate racism, if I myself and
other former Muslims can change, if young whites
can change, then there is hope for America. It was
certainly strange to find myself, while steeped in the
doctrine that all whites were devils by nature, com-

manded by the heart to applaud and acknowledge respect for these young whites – despite the fact that they are descendants of the masters and I the descendant of slaves. The sins of the fathers are visited upon the heads of the children – but only if the children continue in the evil deeds of the fathers.

NOTES ON A NATIVE SON

After reading a couple of James Baldwin's books, I began experiencing that continuous delight one feels upon discovering a fascinating, brilliant talent on the scene, a talent capable of penetrating so profoundly into one's own little world that one knows oneself to have been unalterably changed and *liberated*, liberated from the frustrating grasp of whatever devils happen to possess one. Being a Negro, I have found this to be a rare and infrequent experience, for few of my black brothers and sisters here in America have achieved the power, which James Baldwin calls his revenge, which outlasts kingdoms: the power of doing whatever cats like Baldwin do when combining the alphabet with the volatile elements of his soul. (And, like it or not, a black man, unless he has become irretrievably 'white-minded', responds with an additional dimension of his being to the articulated experience of another black – in spite of the universality of human experience.)

I, as I imagine many others did and still do, lusted for anything that Baldwin had written. It would have been a gas for me to sit on a pillow beneath the womb of Baldwin's typewriter and catch each newborn page as it entered this world of ours. I was delighted that Baldwin, with those great big eyes of his, which one thought to be fixedly focused on the macrocosm, could also pierce the microcosm. And although he was so full of sound, he was not a noisy writer like

Ralph Ellison He placed so much of my own experience, which I thought I had understood, into new perspective.

Gradually, however, I began to feel uncomfortable about something in Baldwin. I was disturbed upon becoming aware of an aversion in my heart to part of the song he sang. Why this was so, I was unable at first to say. Then I read *Another Country*, and I knew why my love for Baldwin's vision had become ambivalent.

Long before, I had become a student of Norman Mailer's *The White Negro*, which seemed to me to be prophetic and penetrating in its understanding of the psychology involved in the accelerating confrontation of black and white in America. I was therefore personally insulted by Baldwin's flippant, schoolmarmish dismissal of *The White Negro*. Baldwin committed a literary crime by his arrogant repudiation of one of the few gravely important expressions of our time. *The White Negro* may contain an excess of esoteric verbal husk, but one can forgive Mailer for that because of the solid kernel of truth he gave us. After all, it is the baby we want and not the blood of afterbirth. Mailer described, in that incisive essay, the first important chinks in the 'mountain of white supremacy' – important because it shows the depth of ferment, on a personal level, in the white world. People are feverishly, and at great psychic and social expense, seeking *fundamental and irrevocable liberation* – and, what is more important, *are succeeding in escaping* – from the big white lies that compose the monolithic myth of White Supremacy/Black Inferiority, in a desperate attempt on the part of a new generation of white Americans to enter into the cosmopolitan egalitarian spirit of the twentieth century.

75

But let us examine the reasoning that lies behind Baldwin's attack on Mailer.

There is in James Baldwin's work the most grueling, agonizing, total hatred of the blacks, particularly of himself, and the most shameful, fanatical, fawning, sycophantic love of the whites that one can find in the writings of any black American writer of note in our time. This is an appalling contradiction and the implications of it are vast.

A re-reading of *Nobody Knows My Name* cannot help but convince the most avid of Baldwin's admirers of the hatred for blacks permeating his writings. In the essay 'Princes and Powers', Baldwin's antipathy toward the black race is shockingly clear. The essay is Baldwin's interpretation of the Conference of Black Writers and Artists which met in Paris in September 1956. The portrait of Baldwin that comes through his words is that of a mind in unrelenting opposition to the efforts of solemn, dedicated black men who have undertaken the enormous task of rejuvenating and reclaiming the shattered psyches and culture of the black people, a people scattered over the continents of the world and the islands of the seas, where they exist in the mud of the floor of the foul dungeon into which the world has been transformed by the whites.

In his report of the conference, Baldwin, the reluctant black, dragging his feet at every step, could only ridicule the vision and efforts of these great men and heap scorn upon them, reserving his compliments – all of them left-handed – for the speakers at the conference who were themselves rejected and booed by the other conferees because of their reactionary, sycophantic views. Baldwin felt called upon to pop his cap pistol in a duel with Aimé Césaire, the big gun from Martinique. Indirectly, Baldwin was defending his first love – the white man. But the revulsion which Baldwin felt for the blacks at this conference, who were glorying in their blackness, seeking and showing their pride in Negritude and the African Personality, drives him to self-revealing sortie after sortie, so obvious in 'Princes and Powers'. Each successive sortie, however, becomes more expensive than the last one, because to score each time he has to go a little farther out on the limb, and it takes him a little longer each time to hustle back to the cover and camouflage of the perfumed smoke screen of his prose. Now and then we catch a glimpse of his little jive ass – his big eyes peering back over his shoulder in the mischievous retreat of a child sneak-thief from a cookie jar.

In the autobiographical notes of *Notes of a Native Son*, Baldwin is frank to confess that, in growing into his version of manhood in Harlem, he discovered that, since his African heritage had been wiped out and was not accessible to him, he would appropriate the white man's heritage and make it his own. This terrible reality, central to the psychic stance of all American Negroes, revealed to Baldwin that he hated and feared white people. Then he says: 'This did not mean that I loved black people; on the contrary, I despised them, possibly because they failed to produce Rembrandt.' The psychic distance between love and hate could be the mechanical difference between a smile and a sneer, or it could be the journey of a nervous impulse from the depths of one's brain to the tip of one's toe. But this impulse in its path through North American nerves may, if it is honest, find the passage disputed: may find the leap from the fiber of hate to that of love too taxing on its meager store of energy – and so the long trip back may never be completed, may end in a reconnaissance, a compromise, and then a lie.

Self-hatred takes many forms; sometimes it can be detected by no one, not by the keenest observer, not by the self-hater himself, not by his most intimate friends. Ethnic self-hate is even more difficult to detect. But in American Negroes, this ethnic self-hatred often takes the bizarre form of a racial death-wish, with many and elusive manifestations. Ironically, it provides much of the impetus behind the motivations of integration. And the attempt to suppress or deny such drives in one's psyche leads many American Negroes to become ostentatious separationists, Black Muslims, and back-to-Africa advocates. It is no wonder that Elijah Muhammad could conceive of the process of controlling evolution whereby the white race was brought into being. According to Elijah, about 6300 years ago all the people of the earth were Original Blacks. Secluded on the island of Patmos, a mad black scientist by the name of Yacub set up the machinery for grafting whites out of blacks through the operation of a birth-control system. The population on this island of Patmos was 59,999 and whenever a couple on this island wanted to get married they were only allowed to do so if there was a difference in their color, so that by mating black with those in the population of a brownish color and brown with brown – but never black with black – all traces of the black were eventually eliminated; the process was repeated until all the brown was eliminated, leaving only men of the red race; the red was bleached out, leaving only yellow; then the yellow was bleached out, and only white was left. Thus Yacub, who was long since dead, because this whole process took hundreds of years, had finally succeeded in creating the white devil with the blue eyes of death.

This myth of the creation of the white race, called 'Yacub's History', is an inversion of the racial death-wish of American Negroes. Yacub's plan is still being followed by many Negroes today. Quite simply, many Negroes believe, as the principle of assimilation into white America implies, that the race problem in America cannot be settled until all traces of the black race are eliminated. Toward this end, many Negroes loathe the very idea of two very dark Negroes mating. The children, they say, will come out ugly. What they mean is that the children are sure to be black, and this is not desirable. From the widespread use of cosmetics to bleach the black out of one's skin and other concoctions to take Africa out of one's hair, to the extreme, resorted to by more Negroes than one might wish to believe, of undergoing nose-thinning and lip-clipping operations, the racial death-wish of American Negroes – Yacub's goal – takes its terrible toll. What has been happening for the past four hundred years is that the white man, through his access to black women, has been pumping his blood and genes into the blacks, has been diluting the blood and genes of the blacks – i.e., has been fulfilling Yacub's plan and accelerating the Negroes' racial death-wish.

The case of James Baldwin aside for a moment, it seems that many Negro homosexuals, acquiescing in this racial death-wish, are outraged and frustrated because in their sickness they are unable to have a baby by a white man. The cross they have to bear is that, already bending over and touching their toes for the white man, the fruit of their miscegenation is not the little half-white offspring of their dreams but an increase in the unwinding of their nerves – though they redouble their efforts and intake of the white man's sperm.

In this land of dichotomies and disunited opposites, those truly concerned with the resurrection of black Americans have had eternally to deal with black intellectuals who have become their own opposites, taking on all of the behavior patterns of their enemy, vices and virtues, in an effort to aspire to alien standards in all respects. The gulf between an audacious, boot-licking Uncle Tom and an intellectual buckdancer is filled only with sophistication and style. On second thought, Uncle Tom comes off much cleaner here because usually he is just trying to survive, choosing to pretend to be something other than his true self in order to please the white man and thus receive favors. Whereas the intellectual sycophant does not pretend to be other than he actually is, but hates what he is and seeks to redefine himself in the image of his white idols. He becomes a white man in a black body. A self-willed, automated slave, he becomes the white man's most valuable tool in oppressing other blacks.

The black homosexual, when his twist has a racial nexus, is an extreme embodiment of this contradiction. The white man has deprived him of his masculinity, castrated him in the center of his burning skull, and when he submits to this change and takes the white man for his lover as well as Big Daddy, he focuses on 'whiteness' all the love in his pent-up soul and turns the razor edge of hatred against 'blackness' – upon himself, what he is, and all those who look like him, remind him of himself. He may even hate the darkness of night.

The racial death-wish is manifested as the driving force in James Baldwin. His hatred for blacks, even as he pleads what he conceives as their cause, makes him the apotheosis of the dilemma in the ethos of the black bourgeoisie who have completely rejected their African heritage, consider the loss irrevocable, and refuse to look again in that direction. This is the root of Baldwin's violent repudiation of Mailer's *The White Negro*.

To understand what is at stake here, and to understand it in terms of the life of this nation, is to know the central fact that the relationship between black and white in America is a power equation, a power struggle, and that this power struggle is not only manifested in the aggregate (civil rights, black nationalism, etc.) but also in the interpersonal relationships, actions, and reactions between blacks and whites where taken into account. When those 'two lean cats', Baldwin and Mailer, met in a French living-room, it was precisely this power equation that was at work.

It is fascinating to read (in *Nobody Knows My Name*) in what terms this power equation was manifested in Baldwin's immediate reaction to that meeting: 'And here we were, suddenly, circling around each other. We liked each other at once, but each was frightened that the other would pull rank. He could have pulled rank on me because he was more famous and *had more money* and also *because he was white*; but I could have pulled rank on him precisely because I was black and knew more about that periphery he so helplessly maligns in *The White Negro* than he could ever hope to know.' [Italics added.]

F

Pulling rank, it would seem, is a very dangerous business, especially when the troops have mutinied and the basis of one's authority, or rank, is devoid of that interdictive power and has become suspect. One would think that for Baldwin, of all people, these hues of black and white were no longer armed with the power to intimidate – and if one thought this, one would be exceedingly wrong: for behind the structure of the thought of Baldwin's quoted above, there lurks the imp of Baldwin's unwinding, of his tension between love and hate – love of the white and hate of the black. And when we dig into this tension we will find that when those 'two lean cats' crossed tracks in that French living-room, one was a Pussy Cat, the other a Tiger. Baldwin's purr was transmitted magnificently in *The Fire Next Time*. But his work is the fruit of a tree with a poison root. Such succulent fruit, such a painful tree, what a malignant root!

It is ironic, but fascinating for what it reveals about the ferment in the North American soul in our time, that Norman Mailer, the white boy, and James Baldwin, the black boy, encountered each other in the eye of a social storm, traveling in opposite directions; the white boy, with knowledge of white Negroes, was traveling toward a confrontation with the black, with Africa; while the black boy, with a white mind, was on his way to Europe. Baldwin's nose, like the North-seeking needle on a compass, is for ever pointed toward his adopted fatherland, Europe, his by intellectual osmosis and in Africa's stead. What he says of Aimé Césaire, one of the greatest black writers of the twentieth century, and intending it as an ironic re-buke, that 'he had penetrated into the heart of the great wilderness which was Europe and stolen the sacred fire ... which ... was ... the assurance of his power', seems only too clearly to speak more about Peter than it does about Paul. What Baldwin seems to forget is that Césaire explains that fire, whether sacred or profane, burns. In Baldwin's case, though the fire could not burn the black off his face, it certainly did burn it out of his heart.

I am not interested in denying anything to Baldwin. I, like the entire nation, owe a great debt to him. But throughout the range of his work, from *Go Tell It on the Mountain*, through *Notes of a Native Son*, *Nobody Knows My Name*, *Another Country*, to *The Fire Next Time*, all of which I treasure, there is a decisive quirk in Baldwin's vision which corresponds to his relationship to black people and to masculinity. It was this same quirk, in my opinion, that compelled Baldwin to slander Rufus Scott in *Another Country*, venerate André Gide, repudiate *The White Negro*, and drive the blade of Brutus into the corpse of Richard Wright. As Baldwin has said in *Nobody Knows My Name*, 'I think that I know something about the American masculinity which most men of my generation do not know because they have not been menaced by it in the way I have been.' O.K., Sugar, but isn't it true that Rufus Scott, the weak, craven-hearted ghost of *Another Country*, bears the same relation to Bigger Thomas of *Native Son*, the black rebel of the ghetto and a man, as you yourself bore to the fallen giant, Richard Wright, a rebel and a man?

Somewhere in one of his books, Richard Wright describes an encounter between a ghost and several young Negroes. The young Negroes rejected the homosexual, and this was Wright alluding to a classic, if cruel, example of a ubiquitous phenomenon in the black ghettos of America: the practice by Negro youths of going 'punk-hunting'. This practice of seeking out homosexuals on the prowl, rolling them, beating them up, seemingly just to satisfy some savage impulse to inflict pain on the specific target selected, the 'social outcast', seems to me to be not unrelated, in terms of the psychological mechanisms involved, to the ritualistic lynchings and castrations inflicted on Southern blacks by Southern whites. This was, as I recall, one of Wright's few comments on the subject of homosexuality.

I think it can safely be said that the men in Wright's books, albeit shackled with a form of impotence, were strongly heterosexual. Their heterosexuality was implied rather than laboriously stated or emphasized; it was taken for granted, as we all take men until something occurs to make us know otherwise. And Bigger Thomas, Wright's greatest creation, was a man in violent, though inept, rebellion against the stifling, murderous, totalitarian white world. There was no trace in Bigger of a Martin Luther King-type self-effacing love for his oppressors. For example, Bigger would have been completely baffled, as most Negroes are today, at Baldwin's advice to his nephew (*The Fire Next Time*), concerning white people: 'You must accept them *and accept them with love*. For these innocent people have no other hope.' [Italics added.]

Rufus Scott, a pathetic wretch who indulged in the white man's pastime of committing suicide, who let a white bisexual homosexual fuck him in his ass, and who took a Southern Jezebel for his woman, with all that these tortured relationships imply, was the epitome of a black eunuch who has completely submitted to the white man. Yes, Rufus was a psychological freedom rider, turning the ultimate cheek, murmuring like a ghost, *'You took the best so why not take the rest,'* which has absolutely nothing to do with the way Negroes have managed to survive here in the hells of North America! This all becomes very clear from what we learn of Erich, the arch-ghost of *Another Country*, of the depths of his alienation from his body and the source of his need: 'And it had taken him almost until this very moment, on the eve of his departure, to begin to recognize that part of Rufus' great power over him had to do with the past which Erich had buried in some deep, dark place; was connected with himself, in Alabama, *when I wasn't nothing but a child*; with the cold white people and the warm black people, warm at least for him ...'

So, too, who cannot wonder at the source of such audacious madness as moved Baldwin to make this startling remark about Richard Wright, in his ignoble essay 'Alas, Poor Richard': 'In my own relations with him, I was always exasperated by his notions of society, politics, and history, for they seemed to me utterly fanciful. I never believed that he had any real sense of how a society is put together.'

Richard Wright is dead and Baldwin is alive and with us. Baldwin says that Richard Wright held notions that were utterly fanciful, and Baldwin is an honorable man.

O Judgment! thou art fled to brutish beasts,
And men have lost their reason.

Wright has no need, as Caesar did, of an outraged Antony to plead his cause: his life and his work are his shield against the mellow thrust of Brutus' blade The good that he did, unlike Caesar's, will not be interred with his bones. It is, on the contrary, only the living who can be harmed by Brutus.

Baldwin says that in Wright's writings violence sits enthroned where sex should be. If this is so, then it is only because in the North American reality hate holds sway in love's true province. And it is only through a rank perversion that the artist, whose duty is to tell us the truth, can turn the two-dollar trick of wedding violence to love and sex to hate – if, to achieve this end, one has basely to transmute rebellion into lamblike submission – *'You took the best,'* sniveled Rufus, *'so why not take the rest?'* Richard Wright was not ghost enough to achieve this cruel distortion. With him, sex, being not a spectator sport or a panacea but the sacred vehicle of life and love, is itself sacred. And the America which Wright knew and which *is*, is not the Garden of Eden but its opposite. Baldwin, embodying in his art the self-flagellating policy of Martin Luther King, and giving out falsely the news that the Day of the Ghost has arrived, pulled it off in *Another Country*.

Of all black American novelists, and indeed of all American novelists of any hue, Richard Wright reigns supreme for his profound political, economic, and social reference. Wright had the ability, like Dreiser, of harnessing the gigantic, overwhelming environmental forces and focusing them, with pinpoint sharpness, on individuals and their acts as they are caught up in the whirlwind of the savage, anarchistic sweep of life, love, death, and hate, pain, hope, pleasure, and despair across the face of a nation and the world. But, ah! 'O masters', it is Baldwin's work which is so void of a political, economic, or even a social reference. His characters all seem to be fucking and sucking in a vacuum. Baldwin has a superb touch when he speaks of human beings, when he is inside of them – especially his homosexuals – but he flounders when he looks beyond the skin; whereas Wright's forte, it seems to me, was in reflecting the intricate mechanisms of a social organization, its functioning as a unit.

Baldwin's essay on Richard Wright reveals that he despised – not Richard Wright, but his masculinity. He cannot confront the stud in others – except that he must either submit to it or destroy it. And he was not about to bow to a *black* man. Wright understood and lived the truth of what Norman Mailer meant when he said '... for being a man is the continuing battle of one's life, and one loses a bit of manhood with every stale compromise to the authority of any power in which one does not believe'. Baldwin, compromised beyond getting back by the white man's *power*, which is real and which has nothing to do with *authority*, but to which Baldwin has ultimately succumbed psychologically, is totally unable to extricate himself from that horrible pain. It is the scourge of his art, because the only way out for him is psychologically to embrace Africa, the land of his fathers, which he utterly refuses to do. He has instead resorted to a despicable underground guerrilla war, waged on paper, against black masculinity, playing out the racial death-wish of Yacub, reaching, I think, a point where Mailer hits the spot: 'Driven into defiance, it is natural if regrettable, that many homosexuals go to the direction of assuming that there is something intrinsically superior in homosexuality, and carried far enough it is a viewpoint which is as stultifying, as ridiculous, and as anti-human as the heterosexual's prejudice.'

I, for one, do not think homosexuality is the latest advance over heterosexuality on the scale of human evolution. Homosexuality is a sickness, just as are baby-rape or wanting to become the head of General Motors.

A grave danger faces this nation, of which we are as yet unaware. And it is precisely this danger which Baldwin's work conceals; indeed, leads us away from. We are engaged in the deepest, the most fundamental revolution and reconstruction which men have ever been called upon to make in their lives, and which they absolutely cannot escape or avoid except at the peril of the very continued existence of human life on this planet. The time of the sham is over, and the cheek of the suffering saint must no longer be turned twice to the brute. The titillation of the guilt complexes of bored white liberals leads to doom. The grotesque hideousness of what is happening to us is reflected in this remark by Murray Kempton, quoted in *The Realist*: 'When I was a boy Stepin Fetchit was the only Negro actor who worked regularly in the movies ... The fashion changes, but I sometimes think that Malcolm X and, to a degree even James Baldwin, are *our* Stepin Fetchits.'

Yes, the fashion does change. 'Will the machine-gunners please step forward,' said LeRoi Jones in a poem. 'The machine-gun on the corner', wrote Richard Wright, 'is the symbol of the twentieth century.' The embryonic spirit of kamikaze, real and alive, grows each day in the black man's heart and there are dreams of Nat Turner's legacy. The ghost of John Brown is creeping through suburbia. And I wonder if James Chaney said, as Andrew Goodman and Michael Schwerner stood helplessly watching, as the grizzly dogs crushed his bones with savage blows of chains – did poor James say, after Rufus Scott – *'You took the best, so why not take the rest?'* Or did he turn to his white brothers, seeing their plight, and say, after Baldwin, 'That's your problem, baby!'

I say, after Mailer, 'There's a shit-storm coming.'

DOMESTIC LAW AND
INTERNATIONAL ORDER

The police department and the armed forces are the two arms of the power structure, the muscles of control and enforcement. They have deadly weapons with which to inflict pain on the human body. They know how to bring about horrible deaths. They have clubs with which to beat the body and the head. They have bullets and guns with which to tear holes in the flesh, to smash bones, to disable and kill. They use force, to make you do what the deciders have decided you must do.

Every country on earth has these agencies of force. The people everywhere fear this terror and force. To them it is like a snarling wild beast which can put an end to one's dreams. They punish. They have cells and prisons to lock you up in. They pass out sentences. They won't let you go when you want to. You have to stay put until they give the word. If your mother is dying, you can't go to her bedside to say goodbye or to her graveside to see her lowered into the earth, to see her, for the last time, swallowed up by that black hole.

The techniques of the enforcers are many: firing squads, gas chambers, electric chairs, torture chambers, the garrote, the guillotine, the tightening rope around your throat. It has been found that the death penalty is necessary to back up the law, to make it easier to enforce, to deter transgressions against the penal code. That everybody doesn't believe in the same laws is beside the point.

Which laws get enforced depends on who is in power. If the capitalists are in power, they enforce laws designed to protect their system, their way of life. They have a particular abhorrence for crimes against property, but are prepared to be liberal and show a modicum of compassion for crimes against the person – unless, of course, an instance of the latter is combined with an instance of the former. In such cases, nothing can stop them from throwing the whole book at the offender. For instance, armed robbery with violence, to a capitalist, is the very epitome of evil. Ask any banker what he thinks of it.

If Communists are in power, they enforce laws designed to protect their system, their way of life. To them, the horror of horrors is the speculator, that man of magic who has mastered the art of getting something with nothing and who in America would be a member in good standing of his local Chamber of Commerce.

'The people', however, are nowhere consulted, although everywhere everything is done always in their name and ostensibly for their betterment, while their real-life problems go unsolved. 'The people' are a rubber stamp for the crafty and sly. And no problem can be solved without taking the police department and the armed forces into account. Both kings and bookies understand this, as do first ladies and common prostitutes.

The police do on the domestic level what the armed forces do on the international level: protect the way of life of those in power. The police patrol the city, cordon off communities, blockade neighborhoods, invade homes, search for that which is hidden. The armed forces patrol the world, invade countries and continents, cordon off nations, blockade islands and whole peoples; they will also overrun villages, neighborhoods, enter homes, huts, caves, searching for that which is hidden. The policeman and the soldier will violate your person, smoke you out with various gases. Each will shoot you, beat your head and body with sticks and clubs, with rifle butts, run you through with bayonets, shoot holes in your flesh, kill you. They each have unlimited firepower. They will use all that is necessary to bring you to your knees. They won't take no for an answer. If you resist their sticks, they draw their guns. If you resist their guns, they call for reinforcements with bigger guns. Eventually they will come in tanks, in jets, in ships. They will not rest until you surrender or are killed. The policeman and the soldier will have the last word.

Both police and the armed forces follow orders. Orders. Orders flow from the top down. Up there, behind closed doors, in antechambers, in conference rooms, gavels bang on the tables, the tinkling of silver decanters can be heard as icewater is poured by well-fed, conservatively dressed men in horn-rimmed glasses, fashionably dressed American widows with rejuvenated faces and tinted hair, the air permeated with the square humor of Bob Hope jokes. Here all the talking is done, all the thinking, all the deciding. Gray rabbits of men scurry forth from the conference room to spread the decisions throughout the city, as News. Carrying out orders is a job, a way of meeting the payments on the house, a way of providing for one's kiddies. In the armed forces it is also a duty, patriotism. Not to do so is treason.

Every city has its police department. No city would

be complete without one. It would be sheer madness to try operating an American city without the heat, the fuzz, the man. Americans are too far gone, or else they haven't arrived yet; the center does not exist, only the extremes. Take away the cops and Americans would have a coast-to-coast free-for-all. There are, of course, a few citizens who carry their own private cops around with them, built into their souls. But there is robbery in the land, and larceny, murder, rape, burglary, theft, swindles, all brands of crime, profit, rent, interest – and these blasé descendants of Pilgrims are at each other's throats. To complicate matters, there are also rich people and poor people in America. There are Negroes and whites, Indians, Puerto Ricans, Mexicans, Jews, Chinese, Arabs, Japanese – all with equal rights but unequal possessions. Some are haves and some are have-nots. All have been taught to worship at the shrine of General Motors. The whites are on top in America and they want to stay there, up there. They are also on top in the world, on the international level, and they want to stay up there, too. Everywhere there are those who want to smash this precious toy clock of a system, they want ever so much to change it, to rearrange things, to pull the whites down off their high horse and make them equal. Everywhere the whites are fighting to prolong their status, to retard the erosion of their position. In America, when everything else fails, they call out the police. On the international level, when everything else fails, they call out the armed forces.

A strange thing happened in Watts, in 1965, August. The blacks, who in this land of private property have all private and no property, got excited into an uproar because they noticed a cop before he had a chance to wash the blood off his hands. Usually

93

the police department can handle such flare-ups. But this time it was different. Things got out of hand. The blacks were running amok, burning, shooting, breaking. The police department was powerless to control them; the chief called for reinforcements. Out came the National Guard, that ambiguous hybrid from the twilight zone where the domestic army merges with the international; that hypocritical force poised within America and capable of action on either level, capable of backing up either the police or the armed forces. Unleashing their formidable firepower, they crushed the blacks. But things will never be the same again. Too many people saw that those who turned the other cheek in Watts got their whole head blown off. At the same time, heads were being blown off in Vietnam. America was embarrassed, not by the quality of her deeds but by the surplus of publicity focused upon her negative selling points, and a little frightened because of what all those dead bodies, on two fronts, implied. Those corpses spoke eloquently of potential allies and alliances. A community of interest began to emerge, dripping with blood, out of the ashes of Watts. The blacks in Watts and all over America could now see the Viet Cong's point: both were on the receiving end of what the armed forces were dishing out.

So now the blacks, stung by the new knowledge they have unearthed, cry out 'POLICE BRUTALITY!' From one end of the country to the other, the new war cry is raised. The youth, those nodes of compulsive energy who are all fuel and muscle, race their motors, itch to do something. The Uncle Toms, no longer willing to get down on their knees to lick boots, do so from a squatting position. The black bourgeoisie call for Citizens' Review Boards, to assert civilian con-

trol over the activity of the police. In back rooms, in
dark stinking corners of the ghettos, self-conscious
black men curse their own cowardice and stare at their
rifles and pistols and shotguns laid out on tables before them, trembling as they wish for a manly impulse to course through their bodies and send them
screaming mad into the streets shooting from the hip.
Black women look at their men as if they are bugs,
curious growths of flesh playing an inscrutable wait-
ing game. Violence becomes a homing pigeon floating
through the ghettos seeking a black brain in which to
roost for a season.

In their rage against the police, against police
brutality, the blacks lose sight of the fundamental
reality : that the police are only an instrument for the
implementation of the policies of those who make
the decisions. Police brutality is only one facet of the
crystal of terror and oppression. Behind police
brutality there is social brutality, economic brutality,
and political brutality. From the perspective of the
ghetto, this is not easy to discern : the TV newscaster
and the radio announcer and the editorialists of the
newspapers are wizards of the smoke screen and the
snow job.

What is true on the international level is true also
at home; except that the ace up the sleeve is easier to
detect in the international arena. Who would maintain that American soldiers are in Vietnam on their
own motion? They were conscripted into the armed
forces and taught the wisdom of obeying orders. They
were sent to Vietnam by orders of the generals in the
Pentagon, who receive them from the Secretary of
Defense, who receives them from the President, who
is shrouded in mystery. The soldier in the field in
Vietnam, the man who lies in the grass and squeezes

the trigger when a little half-starved, trembling Vietnamese peasant crosses his sights, is only following
orders, carrying out a policy and a plan. He hardly
knows what it is all about. They have him wired-
up tight with the slogans of TV and the World Series.
All he knows is that he has been assigned to carry out
a certain ritual of duties. He is well trained and does
the best he can. He does a good job. He may want to
please those above him with the quality of his performance. He may want to make sergeant, or better. This
man is from some hicky farm in Shit Creek, Georgia.
He only knew whom to kill after passing through boot
camp. He could just as well come out ready to kill
Swedes. He will kill a Swede dead, if he is ordered
to do so.

Same for the policeman in Watts. He is not there on
his own. They have all been assigned. They have been
told what to do and what not to do. They have also
been told what they better not do. So when they continually do something, in every filthy ghetto in this
shitty land, it means only that they are following
orders.

It's no secret that in America the blacks are in
total rebellion against the System. They want to get
their nuts out of the sand. They don't like the way
America is run, from top to bottom. In America,
everything is owned. Everything is held as private
property. Someone has a brand on everything. There
is nothing left over. Until recently, the blacks themselves were counted as part of somebody's private
property, along with the chickens and goats. The
blacks have not forgotten this, principally because
they are still treated as if they are part of somebody's
inventory of assets – or perhaps, in this day of rage
against the costs of welfare, blacks are listed among

the nation's liabilities. On any account, however, blacks are in no position to respect or help maintain the institution of private property. What they want is to figure out a way to get some of that property for themselves, to divert it to their own needs. This is what it is all about, and this is the real brutality involved. This is the source of all brutality.

The police are the armed guardians of the social order. The blacks are the chief domestic victims of the American social order. A conflict of interest exists, therefore, between the blacks and the police. It is not solely a matter of trigger-happy cops, of brutal cops who love to crack black heads. Mostly it's a job to them. It pays good. And there are numerous fringe benefits. The real problem is a trigger-happy social order.

The Utopians speak of a day when there will be no police. There will be nothing for them to do. Every man will do his duty, will respect the rights of his neighbor, will not disturb the peace. The needs of all will be taken care of. Everyone will have sympathy for his fellow man. There will be no such thing as crime. There will be, of course, no prisons. No electric chairs, no gas chambers. The hangman's rope will be the thing of the past. The entire earth will be a land of plenty. There will be no crimes against property, no speculation.

It is easy to see that we are not on the verge of entering Utopia: there are cops everywhere. North and South, the Negroes are the have-nots. They see property all around them, property that is owned by whites. In this regard, the black bourgeoisie has become nothing but a ridiculous nuisance. Having waged a battle for entrance into the American mainstream

continually for fifty years, all of the black bourgeoisie's defenses are directed outward, against the
whites. They have no defenses against the blacks and
no time to erect any. The black masses can handle
them any time they choose, with one mighty blow.
But the white bourgeoisie presents a bigger problem,
those whites who own everything. With many
shackled by unemployment, hatred in black hearts for
this system of private property increases daily. The
sanctity surrounding property is being called into
question. The mystique of the deed of ownership is
melting away. In other parts of the world, peasants
rise up and expropriate the land from the former
owners. Blacks in America see that the deed is not
eternal, that it is not signed by God, and that new
deeds, making blacks the owners, can be drawn up.

The Black Muslims raised the cry, 'WE MUST
HAVE SOME LAND!' 'SOME LAND OF OUR
OWN OR ELSE!' Blacks in America shrink from
the colossus of General Motors. They can't see how
to wade through that thicket of common stocks,
preferred stocks, bonds and debentures. They only
know that General Motors is huge, that it has
billions of dollars under its control, that it owns
land, that its subsidiaries are legion, that it is a
repository of vast powers. The blacks want to
crack the nut of General Motors. They are meditating
on it. Meanwhile, they must learn that the police take
orders from General Motors. And that the Bank of
America has something to do with them even though
they don't have a righteous penny in the bank. They
have no bank accounts, only bills to pay. The only
way they know of making withdrawals from the bank
is at the point of a gun. The shiny fronts of skyscrapers
intimidate them. They do not own them. They feel

alienated from the very sidewalks on which they walk. This white man's country, this white man's world. Overflowing with men of color. An economy consecrated to the succor of the whites. Blacks are incidental. The war on poverty, that monstrous insult of the rippling muscles in a black man's arms, is an index of how men actually sit down and plot each other's deaths, actually sit down with slide rules and calculate how to hide bread from the hungry. And the black bourgeoisie greedily sopping up what crumbs are tossed into their dark corner.

There are 20,000,000 of these blacks in America, probably more. Today they repeat, in awe, this magic number to themselves: there are 20,000,000 of us! They shout this to each other in humiliated astonishment. No one need tell them that there is vast power latent in their mass. They know that 20,000,000 of anything is enough to get some recognition and consideration. They know also that they must harness their number and hone it into a sword with a sharp cutting edge. White General Motors also knows that the unity of these 20,000,000 ragamuffins will spell the death of the system of its being. At all costs, then, they will seek to keep these blacks from uniting, from becoming bold and revolutionary. These white property owners know that they must keep the blacks cowardly and intimidated. By a complex communication system of hints and signals, certain orders are given to the chief of police and the sheriff, who pass them on to their men, the footsoldiers in the trenches of the ghetto.

We experience this system of control as madness. So that Leonard Deadwyler, one of these 20,000,000 blacks, is rushing his pregnant wife to the hospital and is shot dead by a policeman. An accident. That the sun rises in the east and sets in the west is also an accident, by design. The blacks are up in arms. From one end of America to the other, blacks are outraged at this accident, this latest evidence of what an accident-prone people they are, of the cruelty and pain of their lives, these blacks at the mercy of trigger-happy Yankees and Rebs in coalition against their skin. They want the policeman's blood as a sign that the Viet Cong is not the only answer. A sign to save them from the deaths they must die, and inflict. The power structure, without so much as blinking an eye, wouldn't mind tossing Bova to the mob, to restore law and order, but it knows in the vaults of its strength that at all cost the blacks must be kept at bay, that it must uphold the police department, its Guardian. Nothing must be allowed to threaten the set-up. Justice is secondary. Security is the byword.

Meanwhile, blacks are looking on and asking tactical questions. They are asked to die for the System in Vietnam. In Watts they are killed by it. Now – now! – they are asking each other, in dead earnest: Why not die right here in Babylon fighting for a better life, like the Viet Cong? If those little cats can do it, what's wrong with big studs like us?

A mood sets in, spreads across America, across the face of Babylon, jells in black hearts everywhere.

Part Three

WHITE WOMAN, BLACK MAN

THE ALLEGORY OF THE
BLACK EUNUCHS

I sat down to eat my beans at a table for four with
two of my contemporaries: young, strong, superlative
Black Eunuchs in the prime. Soon after we were seated,
an old fat Lazarus, with sleek, grayish hair that had
been artificially straightened and a jolly, ebullient
smile which made him resemble a chocolate Santa
Claus, invited himself over to our table and sat down
in the chair opposite me. I exchanged glances with
my contemporaries. Ironical smiles lit our black faces,
while an intenser fire blazed in our eyes as we
scrutinized this Lazarus interloper.

A few minutes passed in silence.

My contemporaries and I, we had a thing going
about elderly Negroes like this one sitting opposite
from me. There was something in his style, the way
he carried himself, that we held in contempt. We had
him written down as an Uncle Tom – not that we had
ever seen him buck dancing or licking the white man's
boots, but we knew that black rebels his age do not
walk the streets in America: they were either dead,
in prison, or in exile in another country. Or else, and
this is how we sized this one up, they had turned into
a type of fake that proliferates in the Negro ghetto.
Not a passive resister (and he wasn't non-violent), he
was death on another black, and although the white
man had ripped off his whole existence, his whole

race, he was always talking about what he would do if the white man ever did something to him personally. If talk alone could overthrow a government he would be in power. From a certain point of view we hated this black, but in a subtle way we were fascinated by the curious terms at which he had arrived with the world.

Just then, and with no apparent provocation, the young Eunuch on my left said, pounding his fist on the table for emphasis, 'Old Lazarus, why come you're not dead?'

'What?' asked the Infidel, startled more by the suddenness of the question and the menacing tone in which it was hurled at him than by the question itself. (After all, his entire generation was being asked the same question in a million different guises: Charlie Parker asked Lester Young, Dizzy Gillespie asked Louis Armstrong, Mao Tse-tung asked Chiang Kai-shek, Fidel Castro asked Batista, Malcolm X asked Martin Luther King, Robert F. Williams asked Roy Wilkins, Norman Mailer asked the Totalitarian Squares.) The question sank in slowly, and as it did his Santa Claus smile dissolved, with a hint of panic, into a twitch at the left corner of his fat mouth. His dark, beady eyes darted from face to face.

'I asked you why aren't you dead?' repeated the Eunuch on my left.

'Why should *I* be dead? I don't under – '

'If you had laid down your life,' the Eunuch cut him off, 'at least we could respect you. At least we could say you were a man – a great man. At least we could point to your grave as a sign, a standard, with pride – *with reverence*! But no, you cringing cunctator, you dared to cling to your miserable life, to grow old and gray and fat and funky!' The Accuser broke off and started eating his beans with a vengeance, as though each bean were a white man, and he downed them by the spoonful.

'What's wrong with this cat today?' asked the Accused, his face screwed up in nervous bafflement.

'He's sick,' I offered, to see how the Infidel would take it.

'He must be sick,' said the Accused, stirring his coffee uncertainly. 'All this stupid talk about death and dying.'

'Yes, I'm sick!' erupted the Accuser, almost choking, talking through his beans. '*You* make me sick, Methuselah! What are you trying to do, win a longevity contest? How did you get that gray hair – how did you manage to survive? Yeah. I'm sick, sick, sick!'

'I'm sick, too,' said the Eunuch on my right, speaking for the first time. 'I'm sick, sick, sick!'

'I'm sick, too,' I said.

'What's the name of this game?' asked Lazarus, trying to inject a note of levity, on the sly. 'This is a new one on me.'

It was a cruel thing we were doing and we knew it because we had done it before to others. In one sense we were only playing with him, probing him, examining him, studying him, but on another level we were deadly serious. The Lazarus, detecting the ambiguity, was confused.

'Do you know the difference between a *gorilla* and a *guerrilla*?' the Eunuch on my right asked the Accused.

The Accused appeared to be contemplating an answer.

'I'll make it easy for you,' the Eunuch said. 'You're a gorilla, and a guerrilla is everything you are not.'

The Accused opened his mouth to reply, but the Eunuch on my left, who had cast the first stone, cut him off. 'A guerrilla is a man,' he snapped, his eyes flashing, 'but you're some kind of freak!'

A self-searching, inward-looking silence ensued. One thought of blood and guns and knives, whips, ropes and chains and trees, screams, night riders, fear, nightsticks, police dogs and firehoses, fire, wounds and bombs, old women in pain and young women defiled, lies, jeers, little boys frozen in their first heat and young men *de*studded and old men burnt out, little girls psychically vitiated and physically massacred ...

After a while I asked the Accused, in a neutral voice, 'Have you ever hit a black woman?'

As if his switch had been flipped, his eyes lit up and, anxious for what in his death he took to be a change of subject, the Lazarus took the bait. The twinkle in his eye turned evil as he leaned across the table and said, in a confidential way: 'I wish I had a nickel for every bitch whose ass I've put my foot in! I'd be so rich right now that you lames would have to put in your requests six months in advance just to get to see me, let alone sit down at the same table with me!'

'A home-run slash at your neck with a scimitar is the solution to all your problems, Lazarus!' hissed the Accuser, the Eunuch on my left, his lips trembling with rage.

'What do you mean by that?' asked the Accused, affecting not to have understood.

'He means what I mean,' said the Eunuch on my right, 'that for four hundred years you have had the fear of the slavemaster in you, but now it's time for you to know the fear of your own kind!'

'Humph!' snorted the Accused, and he took a spoon-

ful of beans into his mouth, chewing
He resumed talking after a few mon
women take kindness for weakness. Leav
least little opening and they will put you on
I hate a black bitch. You can't trust them li
women, and if you try to, they won't appreciat   d
they won't know how to act. It would be like trying
to pamper a cobra. Anyway, every black woman
secretly hates black men. Secretly, they all love white
men – some of them will tell you so to your face, the
others will tell you by their deeds and actions. Haven't
you ever noticed that just as soon as a black woman
becomes successful she marries a white man? I'm
going by what I know. I know one black bitch who
always says that there ain't nothing a black man can
do for her except leave her alone or bring her a
message from, or carry a message to, a white man.

'There is no love left between a black man and a
black woman. Take me, for instance. I love white
women and hate black women. It's just in me, so deep
that I don't even try to get it out of me any more. I'd
jump over ten nigger bitches just to get to one white
woman. Ain't no such thing as an ugly white woman.
A white woman is beautiful even if she's baldheaded
and only has one tooth ... It's not just the fact that
she's a woman that I love; I love her skin, her soft,
smooth, white skin. I like to just lick her white skin
as if sweet, fresh honey flows from her pores, and
just to touch her long, soft, silky hair. There's a soft-
ness about a white woman, something delicate and
soft inside her. But a nigger bitch seems to be full of
steel, granite-hard and resisting, not soft and submis-
sive like a white woman. Ain't nothing more beautiful
than a white woman's hair being blown by the wind.
The white woman is more than a woman to me ...

...ie's like a goddess, a symbol. My love for her is religious and beyond fulfillment. I worship her. I love a white woman's dirty drawers.

'Sometimes I think that the way I feel about white women, I must have inherited from my father and his father and his father's father – as far back as you can go into slavery. I must have inherited from all those black men part of my desire for the white woman, because I have more love for her than one man should have. Yes, I want all the white women that they wanted but were never able to get. They passed on their desire to me, they must have; desire for the white woman is like a cancer eating my heart out and devouring my brain. In my dreams I see white women jumping over a fence like dainty little lambs, and every time one of them jumps over, her hair just catches the breeze and splays out behind her like a mane on a Palomino stallion: blondes, redheads, brunettes, strawberry blondes, dirty blondes, drug-store blondes, platinum blondes – all of them. They are the things in my nightmares. Does all this sound like I'm making it up, youngblood?'

He nodded at me; he was asking me. I took my time about answering. I would have preferred to remain silent. I said, 'Why should you lie to us? I mean, no one can be completely true in all that they say, and you give me the impression of, well, talking off the top of your head ...'

He was laughing inside, I could see it in his eyes. Then he said, 'Well, I've thought about it for years. You have to try to understand what's bugging you, you know. But really, I don't believe that I understand anything about anything, when you get right down to it. But I'm stuck with myself and I accept my own thoughts about things. For instance, I don't know just how it works, I mean I can't analyse it, but I know that the white man made the black woman the symbol of slavery and the white woman the symbol of freedom. Every time I embrace a black woman I'm embracing slavery, and when I put my arms around a white woman, well, I'm hugging freedom. The white man forebade me to have the white woman on pain of death. Literally, if I touched a white woman it would cost me my life. Men die for freedom, but black men die for white women, who are the symbol of freedom. That was the white man's will, and as long as he has the power to enforce his will upon me, force me to submit to his will in this instance or in any other, I will not be free. I will not be free until the day I can have a white woman in my bed and a white man minds his own business. Until that day comes, my entire existence is tainted, poisoned, and I will still be a slave – and so will the white woman.

'You may not believe this … when I mount a nigger bitch, I close my eyes and concentrate real hard, and pretty soon I get to believing that I'm riding one of them bucking blondes. I tell you the truth, that's the only way that I can bust my nuts with a black bitch, to close my eyes and pretend that she is Jezebel. If I was to look down and see a black bitch underneath me or if my hand happened to feel her nappy hair, that would be the end, it would be all over. I might as well get on up and split because I wouldn't be able to get anything down, even if I piled her all night long. Any black man who says he don't dig Jezebel is a goddam liar. I believe that if a leader wanted to unite the Negroes in a solid unity, he could do so very easily. All he'd have to do is promise every black man a white woman and every black woman a white man.

He would have so many followers that he wouldn't know what to do with them all. Believe me.

'I'm going to tell you three youngbloods something that I don't like to talk about. I don't like to talk about none of this shit ... You cats are sitting here all puffed up. You think you got a hell of a thing going for yourselves, but you don't really know anything about yourselves, or about your women, or about white people. You probably won't believe what I tell you: it rubs your ego the wrong way. But I'm going to tell you anyway.'

The Lazarus paused and squirmed around in his chair as though trying to get a better grip on it with his rump. When he spoke again there was a tremor in his voice: 'He who worships the Virgin Mary will lust for the beautiful dumb blonde. And she who yearns to be rocked in the arms of Jesus will burn for the blue eyes and white arms of the All-American Boy.'

Here the Lazarus stopped and searched our faces. But our faces were impenetrable masks and we gave him no sign. He went on: 'The war going on between the black man and the white man is not the only war. Life is full of little wars and you fight them all at the same time. You have to have a grand strategy designed to cope with all hostilities, you have to have a style, and if there is someone making war on you and you don't know it, well, you are in big trouble, you're lost from the go ... There is a war going on between the black man and the black woman, which makes her the silent ally, indirectly but effectively, of the white man. The black woman is an unconsenting ally and she may not even realize it – but the white man sure does. That's why, all down through history, he has propped her up economically above you and me, to strengthen her hand against us. But the white man is a fool because he is also fighting a war against the white woman. And it doesn't end there: white men have a war going on against each other.

'The myth of the strong black woman is the other side of the coin of the myth of the beautiful dumb blonde. The white man turned the white woman into a weak-minded, weak-bodied, delicate freak, a sex pot, and placed her on a pedestal; he turned the black woman into a strong self-reliant Amazon and deposited her in his kitchen – that's the secret of Aunt Jemima's bandanna. The white man turned himself into the Omnipotent Administrator and established himself in the Front Office. And he turned the black man into the Supermasculine Menial, and kicked him out into the fields. The white man wants to be the *brain* and he wants us to be the muscle, the *body*. All this is tied up together in a crazy way which was never too clear to me. At one time it seems absolutely clear and at other times I don't believe in it. It reminds me of two sets of handcuffs that have all four of us tied up together, holding all black and white flesh in a certain mold. This is why, when you get down to the root of it, the white man doesn't want the black man, the black woman, or the white woman to have a higher education. Their enlightenment would pose a threat to his omnipotence.

'Haven't you ever wondered why the white man genuinely applauds a black man who achieves excellence with his body in the field of sports, while he hates to see a black man achieve excellence with his brain? The mechanics of the myth demand that the Brain and the Body, like east and west, must never meet – especially in competition on the same level. When it comes to the mechanics of the myth, the

Brain and the Body are mutually exclusive. There can be no true competition between superiors and inferiors. This is why it has been so hard historically for Negroes to break the color bar in sport after sport. Once the color bar falls, the magic evaporates, and when the black man starts to excel in a particular sport the question starts floating around: "Is boxing dying?" "Is baseball through?" "What happened to football?" "What is basketball coming to?" In fact, the new symbol of white supremacy is golf, because there the Brain dominates the Body. But just as soon as the Body starts ripping off a few trophies, they will be asking the question, "What happened to golf?"

'All this became clear when Joe Louis cleaned out Max Schmeling in their second fight. Schmeling stood for the very thing the white man nursed and worshiped in his own heart. But the whites applauded Joe for crushing Schmeling. Why? Because Joe's victory over Schmeling symbolized the triumph of capitalistic democracy over Nazism? No! There may have been a little of that to it, but on a deeper level they applauded Joe for the same reason they despised Ingemar Johansson, while rewarding him handsomely, for knocking out Floyd Patterson. Joe's victory over Schmeling confirmed, while Floyd's defeat contradicted, the white man's image of the black man as the Supermasculine Menial, the personification of mindless brute force, the perfect slave. And Sonny Liston, the mindless Body, is preferred over loud-mouthed Cassius Clay, because, after all, it takes at least a birdbrain to run a loud mouth, and the white man despises even that much brain in a black man. And when Clay, the loud-mouthed clown, abdicates his image as the Body and becomes Muhammad Ali, the Brain, whitey can't hold his mud! The white man loves the Super-masculine Menial – John Henry, the steel-driving man, all Body, driven to his knees by the Machine, which is the phallus symbol of the Brain and the ultimate ideal of the Omnipotent Administrator. To the white man's way of thinking, this was a perfect system of social imagery. But like all perfect systems, it had a great big flaw right in the middle of it.

'The Omnipotent Administrator conceded to the Super-masculine Menial all of the attributes of masculinity associated with the Body: strength, brute power, muscle, even the beauty of the brute body. Except one. There was this single attribute of masculinity which he was unwilling to relinquish, even though this particular attribute is the essence and seat of masculinity: sex. The penis. The black man's penis was the monkey wrench in the white man's perfect machine. The penis, virility, is of the Body. It is not of the Brain: the Brain is neuter, *homo, machine*. But in the deal which the white man forced upon the black man, the black man was given the Body as his domain while the white man pre-empted the Brain for himself. By and by, the Omnipotent Administrator discovered that in the fury of his scheming he had blundered and clipped himself of his penis. (Notice the puny image the white man has of his own penis. He calls it a "prick", a "peter", a "pecker".) So he reneged on the bargain. He called the Supermasculine Menial back and said: "Look, Boy, we have a final little adjustment to make. I'm still going to be the Brain and you're still the Body. But from now on, you do all the flexing but I'll do all the fucking. The Brain must control the Body. To prove my omnipotence I must cuckold you and fetter your bull balls. I will fetter the range of your rod and limit its reach. My

H 113

prick will excel your rod. I have made a calculation. I will have sexual freedom. But I will bind your rod with my omnipotent will, and place a limitation on its aspiration which you will violate on pain of death ... I will have access to the white woman and I will have access to the black woman. The black woman will have access to you – but she will also have access to me. I forbid you access to the white woman. The white woman will have access to me, the Omnipotent Administrator, but I deny her access to you, you, the Supermasculine Menial. By subjecting your manhood to the control of my will, I shall control you. The stem of the Body, the penis, must submit to the will of the Brain."

'It was the perfect solution, only it didn't work. It only drove the truth underground. You can't really dissociate the penis from the Body! Not even the Brain, the Omnipotent Administrator, can do that! *But you can seize the Body in a rage, in violent and hateful frustration at this one great flaw in a perfect plan, this monkey wrench in a perfect machine, string the Body from the nearest tree and pluck its strange fruit, its big Nigger dick, pickle it in a bottle and take it home to the beautiful dumb blonde and rejoice in the lie that not the Body but the Brain is the man.*'

The Lazarus stopped talking and sat there with his mouth hanging open. He was breathing hard, as if he had been running and was out of breath. The Eunuch on my left was staring off into space, looking off deliberately rather than allow anyone to see the wild look I knew would be in his eyes. Thought refused to crystallize in my mind; I poured more coffee into my cup, and as I lifted the cup to my lips I blew softly on the surface of the murky brew to cool it off, and stared over the rim at the Infidel, who sat with his face screwed up, biting his ample bottom lip, as if he was trying hard to remember something or maybe to understand or figure something out. He seemed embarrassed. The Eunuch on my right was staring down into his plate of beans.

Then the Infidel looked up and locked my eyes with his own. A cruel, wounded expression was in his eyes. I could see a pain there that was dreadful. It made me feel fear – not so much for the Infidel as for myself, my generation, my contemporaries, because I was not sure that I, we, knew what to do or would learn before it was too late, and would be able to escape from feeling that same deep-seated pain some day, myself, ourselves. It seemed to me in that moment, and I knew that the same thought was running through the minds of my Eunuch contemporaries, that any fate, death, the gas chamber, the electric chair, a firing squad, heroin, suicide – anything would be better than to submit to the terrible, horrible pain which the Infidel had learned to live with. I felt a hot throbbing in my crotch. Instinctively and with a taste of panic, I reached down, almost afraid that my rod would be missing, but it was there and it was erect and I squeezed it and it was strong and resilient and firm. When I gave it that squeeze, a wave of strength surged through my body. I felt powerful, and I knew that I would make it if I never betrayed the law of my rod. The Infidel smiled, and I was sure he had read my thoughts. He let out a deep breath and sat back in his chair and started talking in a tired voice, almost a monotone:

'I had a woman once – no, *a bitch*! – who had a hook like Sugar Ray Robinson. I had to knock her out every Saturday night. She'd start an argument and

then tee off on me, just like a man. How're you supposed to treat a bitch who can't live with you without fighting? And she didn't have to be mad at me
to start a fight. I experimented with her. I tried all
kinds of technique on her. Once I refused to argue
with her. I just stood there and looked at her in a
way that she knew that I was not mad at her, as if I
was saying to her, "Look, baby, it's up to you. Whatever happens will be because you made it happen."
BOOM! She hit me in the mouth. That was when I
realized that she could not accept me as a man unless
I acted like the Body, exerting physical force over
her. I didn't hit her back. I was filled with a rage that
I had never felt before or since. Actually, I think I
went momentarily insane. I grabbed her by her arm,
whipped out my switchblade knife – it had about an
eight-inch blade – I opened my knife and made her sit
on the sofa. I could see that she thought it was all
over for her. Her eyes were big as a cow's and she
was really scared. I shoved the knife into her hand
and made her take it. Then I lay down with my arms
around her body and with my head in her lap. She
was furious. She threatened to cut my jugular vein if
I did not get up. I was not my usual self and I had no
intention of getting up. It seemed that if I got up I
would not be able to live another second. That was
the feeling I had, that if I got up and let her go or
tried to protect myself in any way from the knife, I
could not go on living. So I laid there with my jugular
vein exposed to her and the knife. And I went to
sleep. At first she tried to get my head out of her lap,
then she stopped that, then she started crying. I could
feel the sobs racking her body. But I kept my eyes
closed and went to sleep. I had no dream or anything.
It was a deep, peaceful, sweet sleep. I can still recall

the ecstasy of that sleep. I have never in my life experienced such blissful sleep. When I woke up, she was holding my head cradled in her lap and she had a beautiful, saintly glow on her face, an expression that was utterly foreign to anything that I had ever seen in her before. Then I remembered the knife and a great fear came over me. I jumped up and looked around. She had closed up the knife and broken the blade and thrown it across the room on the floor. My stomach trembled as I realized what a big chance I had taken.

'Anyway, we went along fine for about a month. Our relationship was infused with new life and vitality. During that time we did not have a single argument, not a single harsh word passed between us. That granite, that steel (which I hate in a black bitch!) was gone. And strangely, I felt myself acting natural, without pretense toward her. It seemed as if we were dancing through those days perfectly in time and in step with each other. Then one day, we were out driving and I ran through a red light just a little too late and this motor-cycle cop pulled me over.

' "Say, Boy," he said to me, "are you color-blind?" I didn't want a ticket so I decided to talk him out of it. I went into my act, gave him a big smile and explained to him that I was awfully sorry, that I thought that I could make it but that my old car was too slow. He talked real bad to me, took me on a long trip about how important it was that I obeyed the laws and regulations and how else can a society be controlled and administered without obedience to the law. I said a bunch of Yes Sir's and No Sir's and he told me to run along and be a good boy. When I drove off, I looked over at my woman and she had turned completely sour. That sweetness of the last month was gone and I could see the granite and steel in her. When we got home she tried to start a fight with me, but I refused to respond. Without another word, she packed up all her belongings and split. The bitch cut me clean aloose. I've never been cut loose that clean before! She got herself another stud. They used to fight all up and down the streets. That stud used to love to fight her just as much as she loved to fight. They were very happy together. Later on, she killed that cat. Shot him down in the street like a dog – and she beat the case in court. They called it justifiable homicide.

'Then the bitch changed her name and started singing professionally. She made it real big, her name and picture was in all the magazines and newspapers. I used to go check her performances in night clubs. She was great. She made a lot of big money. Then guess what she did. She married a white man! The cat was a blank, a tramp, he didn't have anything going for himself. He didn't have a quarter when he married her. She gave him all of her money. He ran through her bank account. He bought himself a big fancy night club. Then he divorced her. She lost her touch after that and started slipping down, down, down. Her earning power shrank to nothing. She hung the whole life up and started singing church music. Spirituals. She joined a church, became real religious. Everybody said she fell in love with Jesus and that in him she finally found her righteous man. That's where she is right now, in that church.

'Ever since then I always believed that marrying a white man ... to a black woman ... is like adding the final star to her crown. It's the apex of achievement in her eyes and in the eyes of her sisters. Look at how many famous black celebrities marry white men. All of the Negro women who are not celebrities wish they were so that they, too, could marry white men.

Whitey is their dream boy. When they kiss you it ain't you they're kissing. They close their eyes and picture their white dream boy. Listen to the grapevine … Jesus Christ the pure is the black woman's psychic bridegroom. You will learn before you die that during coition and at the moment of her orgasm, the black woman, in the first throes of her spasm, shouts out the name of Jesus. "Oh, Jesus, I'm coming!" she shouts to him. And to you it will hurt. It will be like a knife in your heart. It will be the same as if your woman, during orgasm, calls out the name of some sneaky cat who lives down the block.

'Now there is one thing I want to tell you that is directly related to this. To be sure, I have never understood it and I don't believe that I ever will. But I have seen it work and it may be that you brothers can understand it, and it may prove useful to you, it may help you to make it. There is a sickness in the whites that lies at the core of their madness and this sickness makes them act in many different ways. But there is one way it makes some of them act that seems to contradict everything we know about whitey and shakes many blacks up when they first encounter it … There are white men who will pay you to fuck their wives. They approach you and say, "How would you like to fuck a white woman?" "What is this?" you ask. "On the up-and-up," he assures you. "It's all right. She's my wife. She needs black rod, is all. She has to have it. It's like a medicine or drug to her. She has to have it. I'll pay you. It's all on the level, no trick involved. Interested?" You go with him and he drives you to their home. The three of you go into the bedroom. There is a certain type who will leave you and his wife alone and tell you to pile her real good. After it is all over, he will pay you and drive you to wherever you want to go. Then there are some who like to peep at you through a keyhole and watch you have his woman, or peep at you through a window, or lie under the bed and listen to the creaking of the bed as you work out. There is another type who likes to masturbate while he stands beside the bed and watches you pile her. There is the type who likes to eat his woman up after you get through piling her. And there is the type who only wants you to pile her for a little while, just long enough to thaw her out and kick her motor over and arouse her to heat, then he wants you to jump off real quick and he will jump on to her and together they can make it from there by themselves.'

It did not occur to me to say anything; I didn't know what to say. I was angry at the Infidel and repulsed by his monologue and the importance he seemed to attach to these matters. My dreams lay elsewhere and I could not begin to evaluate the things he had been talking about. I sat there, savoring the strange quality of the emotion which had been aroused within me. I don't know when the Eunuch on my left started to speak, for I first became aware of his voice as sound purely, a nebulous, incoherent sound, and only later did I begin to distinguish the words:

' ... fed up with it! You old Lazarus. Everything you said was twisted, it was all dead and stinking, it was all warped and out of joint, it was off cue, off center.' The Eunuch had his jaw set defiantly.

'Yes, I know,' said the Infidel, 'and you youngbloods see your big chance coming up to change all of that. Every man with a pipe dream sees his chance as just coming ... But even so, you have to admit that the white man is a bitch with his shit. Did he clean us out or not, huh? Did he take care of business? He took care of so much business that it got good to him, and he got carried away and cleaned everybody out – including himself. Now ain't that a motherfucking shame?' The Infidel looked from one to the other of us. No one replied to him. We just stared at him, at his face, his eyes, his smooth chocolate skin. Then he broke out laughing, until his obese frame shook. There was no telling what he was laughing at. It was coming from deep inside him, but his face looked pained, as if he were not enjoying his laugh. Several times he tried to say something but each time he was overcome by laughter. Finally he blurted out: ' ... you've got to give the devil his due', and went into another spasm of chuckles and grunts.

When the laughter died he began drumming on the table with his short, fat fingers. 'I had a very close friend once,' he said. 'We grew up together – never mind where. He was the best friend I ever had, closer than a brother. We were tighter than fish pussy, and that's waterproof. When we were just kids, we took a blood-brother oath, like Indian braves. Just me and him. We made a pact to be lifelong comrades.' His mind drifted for a moment. Tiny drops of perspiration stood out on his forehead. 'But something happened and I ... I ... went away ... I didn't see or hear of him for many, many years. Then, finally, I went back ... to that place. I had to see the old hometown once more. I decided to look up my old friend. After searching for him, it turned out that he was in an institution. A mental institution. He had been there ever since – for all those years. So I went to see him. He had changed completely, so much that I don't believe I would have recognized him, if it were not for his eyes. I'd never forget those eyes, never. He had eyes like they say Jomo Kenyatta has, look right through a brick wall.' The Infidel lifted his hand and pointed at the Eunuch on my left. 'My friend had his eyes, only more so, just like this brother here,' he said. An embarrassed, frightened look showed on his face for a moment, which he quickly suppressed. The Eunuch on my left shifted about in his chair.

'But he recognized me, my friend did,' said the Infidel. 'Immediately he knew who I was. He didn't have to pull me from his memory, as you'd think he would have after all those years. The minute they brought him into the visiting room I could see that he recognized me, though he didn't call my name. We sat down at a little table and he said to me : "Ah! I thought you would never get here! Now we can embark on our great enterprise! We will transform the whole of proud Europe into an international whorehouse, and men from all over the earth will make their pilgrimage there and fertilize the depleted human soil with their rich and varied seed!" I said nothing to him, couldn't say anything. I just listened. He talked on and on. He took me back, back, back. Then it was time for me to go. I promised him I'd be back the next day. They led him away. I never went back. Even as I promised him, I knew I would never return, never.' The Infidel paused, swallowed. He was struggling with himself, fighting to keep under control something powerful, torrential, within himself. You could feel the terrible force of the agony raging inside him. 'He died two weeks later, my friend did – from self-inflicted wounds, from banging his own head against a jagged edge of a concrete wall.'

For many minutes no one spoke. Each was submerged in thoughts of his own. Finally, the Eunuch on my left, in a cold, icy tone, said :

'You dirty Lazarus. You killed him. You murdered him. You betrayed him!'

The Infidel made as if to reply, but the effort died. The Eunuch on my left said to the Infidel:

'Your trouble, old Lazarus, is that you can't stand the sight of the slavemaster's blood.'

The Infidel looked surprised. 'The world', he said slowly, 'cannot stand another bloodbath.'

'The world is hemophiliac,' retorted the Eunuch. 'Look at it! When did the world ever stop bleeding? It never has, for a moment, ceased to bleed; it's bleeding somewhere right this very moment. Right now, as we sit here talking, someone somewhere is taking careful aim at someone else, at an enemy. Someone is thrusting with a blade, at an enemy. Someone is lighting a fuse, at an enemy. In Africa, Asia, Europe, South America, and right here in the good old U.S.A., blood is flowing. Go listen to the radio or TV right now and the first news you catch will be of blood, a count of the bodies. Go pick up a newspaper or magazine and it will be dripping with blood. Blood flows from the TV screen. So why does it shock you to hear of blood?'

'Yes, the world is bleeding,' said the Infidel, 'but it's bleeding to death. How much longer can it last?' He shuddered at his own question.

'Blood is a lubricant,' said the Eunuch on my left. 'It smooths the way and enables a people to slip out of the tightest of clutches. You don't tinker with a log-jam, man, you dynamite it!'

'You are thirsty for blood!' said the Infidel, speaking directly to the Eunuch on my left. 'But it won't do!'

'Yes!' replied the Eunuch. 'I'm thirsty for blood – white man's blood. And when I drink I want to drink deeply, because I have a deep thirst to quench. I want to drink for every black man, woman, and child dragged to the slaughter from the shores of Africa, for every one of my brothers and sisters who suffered helplessly in the rotten holds of the damned slave ships – for your friend who bashed his own brains out in that nut-house – I want to drink the white man's blood for every ounce of my flesh and blood that he crushed and broke in the Caribbean Islands, for all the souls of black folk mangled in the fetid fields of the Old South and for every one slaughtered and lynched in the mire of the New South – and in the North, East, and West of the hells of North America! Only the white man's blood can wash away the pain I feel. You shrink from shedding the white man's blood, you old Lazarus, but I say to you that the day is here when I will march into the Mississippi legislature with a blazing machine-gun in my hands and a pocketful of grenades. Since I will be going to die, I definitely will be going to kill.'

'No,' said the Infidel. 'No. More blood will only add crime upon crime. No!' He suddenly stood up from the table, looked at each of us as if to plead, like a criminal before a jury he knows is about to send him to the death chamber. He breathed deeply as he had done earlier, and let his shoulders sag. 'Blood upon blood; crime upon crime; brick of blood upon brick of blood of a new mad Tower of Babel which, too, will fall … There can be no triumph in blood.' Then he turned and faltered slowly away from the table.

We watched him walk away. He stopped and looked back at us, as if he half-expected, half-hoped, for us to call him back. Then he turned and faded from our sight, from our lives.

THE PRIMEVAL MITOSIS

And the Lord God caused a deep sleep to fall upon Adam, and he slept: and he took one of his ribs, and closed up the flesh instead thereof; And the rib, which the Lord God had taken from man, made he a woman, and brought her unto the man. And Adam said, This is now bone of my bones, and flesh of my flesh: she shall be called Woman, because she was taken out of Man.

Genesis II, 21-3

It is as if in the evolution of sex a particle one day broke away from an X-chromosome, and thereafter in relation to X-chromosomes could produce only an incomplete female – the creature we now call the male! It is to this original chromosomal deficiency that all the various troubles to which the male falls heir can be traced.

Ashley Montagu: The Natural Superiority of Women

I think that *any* submerged class is going to be more accustomed to sexuality than a leisure class. A leisure class may be more *preoccupied* with sexuality; but a submerged class is going to be more drenched in it.

You see, the upper classes are obsessed with sex, but they contain very little of it themselves. They use up much too much sex in their manipulations of power. In effect, they exchange sex for power. So they restrict themselves in their sexuality – whereas the submerged classes have to take their desires for power and plow them back into sex.

Norman Mailer: The Presidential Papers

The roots of heterosexuality are buried in that evolutionary choice made long ago in some misty past – but not so remote that it can't be reached with the long arm of the mind – by some unknown forerunner of Homo sapiens. Struggling up from some murky swamp, some stagnant mudhole, some peaceful meadow, that unknown ancestor of Man/Woman, by some weird mitosis of the essence, divided its Unitary Self in half – into the male and female hemispheres of the Primeval Sphere. These hemispheres evolved into what we know today as man and woman.

When the Primeval Sphere divided itself, it established a basic tension of attraction, a dynamic magnetism of opposites – the Primeval Urge – which exerts an irresistible attraction between the male and female hemispheres, ever tending to fuse them back together into a unity in which the male and female realize their true nature – the lost unity of the Primeval Sphere. This is the eternal and unwavering motivation of the male and female hemispheres, of man and woman, to transcend the Primeval Mitosis and achieve supreme identity in the Apocalyptic Fusion.

Each half of the human equation, the male and female hemispheres of the Primeval Sphere, must prepare themselves for the fusion by achieving a Unitary Sexual Image, i.e., a heterosexual identity free from the mutually exclusive, antagonistic, antipodal impediments of homosexuality (the product of the fissure of society into antagonistic classes and a dying culture and civilization alienated from its biology).

Man's continual striving for a Unitary Sexual Image, which can only be achieved in a Unitary Society, becomes a basic driving force of the Class Struggle, which is, in turn, the dynamic of history. The quest for the Apocalyptic Fusion will find optimal conditions only in a Classless Society, the absence of classes being the *sine qua non* for the existence of a Unitary Society in which the Unitary Sexual Image can be achieved.

Each social structure projects on to the screen of possibility the images of the highest type of male and female sexual identities realizable within the limits of that society. The people within that society are motivated and driven, by the perennial quest for Apocalyptic Fusion, to achieve this highest identity, or as close as they can come to the perfection of the Unitary Sexual Image. All impediments to realization of this image become sources of alienation, obstacles in the way of the Self seeking to realize its ultimate identity.

Since each society projects its own sexual image, the Unitary Society will project a Unitary Sexual Image. We can thus postulate, following the model of Marx, that in ancient communal society, which was not cleft into antagonistic classes, there existed a Unitary Society in which a Unitary Sexual Image was in natural coincidence with the way of life of the people. This is the lost innocence of the Garden of Eden.

The Class Society projects a fragmented sexual image. Each class projects a sexual image coinciding with its class-function in society. And since its class-function will differ from that of other classes, its sexual image will differ also and in the same proportion. The source of the fragmentation of the Self in Class Society lies in the alienation between the function of man's Mind and the function of his Body. Man as thinker performs an Administrative Function in society. Man as doer performs a Brute Power Function. These two basic functions I symbolize, when they are embodied in living men functioning in society, as the Omnipotent Administrator and the Supermasculine Menial.

Since all men are created equal, when the Self is fragmented by the operation of the laws and forces of

Class Society, men in the elite classes usurp the controlling and Administrative Function of the society as a whole – i.e., they usurp the administrative component in the nature and biology of the men in the classes below them. Administrative power is concentrated at the apex of society, in the Godhead of the society (pharaoh, king, president, chairman). Administrative power beneath the apex is delegated. Those in classes to which no administrative power has been delegated have the administrative component in their personalities suppressed, alienated, denied expression. Those who have usurped the Administrative Function we shall call the Omnipotent Administrators. Struggling among themselves for higher positions in the administrative hierarchy, they repudiate the component of Brute Power in themselves, claim no kinship with it, and project it on to the men in the classes below them.

All the males in the classes beneath *the* Omnipotent Administrator, or Godhead of the society, are alienated from the administrative component in themselves in proportion to their distance from the apex. That is, they perceive their alienation in terms of their distance from the apex. This perception of their alienation, in terms of the apex, is an illusion. In fact, their alienation must be measured by their distance from the attainment of a Unitary Sexual Image, the take-off stage for the Apocalyptic Fusion. Generally, in a fragmented Class Society, the basic impulse of Omnipotent Administrators is to despise their bodies and glorify their minds.

Those who have been assigned the Brute Power Function we shall call the Supermasculine Menials. They are alienated from their minds. For them the mind counts only in so far as it enables them to receive, understand, and carry out the will of the Omnipotent Administrators.

The Class Society has a built-in bias, which tends to perpetuate the social system. The Omnipotent Administrators, wishing to preserve what they perceive as their superior position and way of life, have, from a class point of view and also on an individual level, a negative reaction toward any influence in the society that tends to increase the number of males qualified to fulfill the functions of administration. When it comes to anything that will better the lot of those beneath him, the Omnipotent Administrator starts with a basic 'anti' reflex. Any liberality he might show is an indication of the extent to which he has suppressed his 'anti' reflex, and is itself a part of his lust for omnipotence. His liberality is, in fact, charity.

The Supermasculine Menial clearly realizes that the superiority of the Omnipotent Administrators over him is based upon the development of their minds and the power they command as a result. Hence, he starts with a 'pro' reflex. He is, for example, pro-universal education at public expense.

Weakness, frailty, cowardice, and effeminacy are, among other attributes, associated with the Mind. Strength, brute power, force, virility, and physical beauty are associated with the Body. Thus the upper classes, or Omnipotent Administrators, are perennially associated with physical weakness, decay, underdeveloped bodies, effeminacy, sexual impotence, and frigidity. Virility, strength, and power are associated with the lower classes, the Supermasculine Menials.

In feudal society, the men of the nobility, who were Omnipotent Administrators by Divine Right, are generally considered to have been weak, delicate, and

I

effeminate, with the affectations of demonstrative homosexuals. The serfs and peasants are considered to have been physically strong, sturdy, hearty, fecund – 'supermasculine'.

The image of the Omnipotent Administrator, that he is markedly effeminate and delicate by reason of his explicit repudiation and abdication of his body in preference for his mind, is decisive for the image of the woman of the elite classes. *Even though her man is effeminate, she is required to possess and project an image that is in sharp contrast to his, more sharply feminine than his, so that the effeminate image of her man can still, by virtue of the sharp contrast in degrees of femininity, be perceived as masculine.* Therefore, she becomes 'Ultrafeminine'.

In order to project an image of Ultrafemininity, the women of the elite repudiate and abdicate the Domestic Function of the female (which is, in the female, the counterpart of the function of Brute Power in the male). To enhance her image and to increase her femininity, the domestic component of her nature is projected on to the women in the classes beneath her, and the femininity of the women below is correspondingly decreased. In effect, a switch is made: the woman of the elite absorbs into her being the femininity of the woman below her, and she extirpates her domestic component; the woman below absorbs the elite woman's cast-off domestic component and relinquishes her own femininity. The elite woman thus becomes 'Ultrafeminine' while the woman below becomes 'Subfeminine'. For the purposes of social imagery, the woman below becomes an Amazon.

Thus, a most weird and complex dialectic of inversion is established in Class Society. The Omnipotent Administrator is launched on a perpetual search for his alienated body, for affirmation of his unstable masculinity. He becomes a worshiper of physical prowess, or he may come to despise the body and everything associated with it. Fearing impotence, impotence being implicit in his negation and abdication of his Body, his profoundest need is for evidence of his virility. His opposite, the Body, the Supermasculine Menial, is a threat to his self-concept (and to compound it all, this perceived threat and resultant fear is reinforced decisively by the fact that the men beneath him are a threat to him *in reality*, because their life goal is to destroy his Omnipotence over them). He views them as his enemies and inferiors, men of a lesser breed than himself and his kind. He despises, hates them. Yet, because of the infirmity in his image and being which moves him to worship masculinity and physical prowess, the Omnipotent Administrator cannot help but covertly, and perhaps in an extremely sublimated guise, envy the bodies and strength of the most alienated men beneath him – those furthest from the apex of administration – because the men most alienated from the mind, least diluted by admixture of the Mind, will be perceived as the most masculine manifestations of the Body: the Supermasculine Menials. (This is precisely the root, the fountainhead, of the homosexuality that is perennially associated with the Omnipotent Administrator.) The dialectic of the Supermasculine Menial is the converse of that of the Omnipotent Administrator. The Supermasculine Menial has an infirmity of the brain because of his alienation from his mind.

Because he despises weakness of the body in himself, the Omnipotent Administrator will have a secret or subconscious aversion to the women of his own class, because of the Ultrafemininity which they have developed to counter-balance his effeminacy. At the same time, he will surpass himself in his efforts to conceal his aversion and make believe that the very opposite is true. He thus makes an icon of his woman and, literally, worships her. He pays obeisance to Her ritualistically while in the chapel of Her presence. Enshrining Her on a pedestal, he goes off seeking confirmation of his insecure masculinity elsewhere. Since the women of the elite tend to become the same, i.e., to project a homogeneous image of Ultrafemininity, they cannot, in the end, satisfy his psychic need – the confirmation of his masculinity. Strength gauges its own potency through a confrontation with other strength. To test it, he must go where it is. He may become addicted to a masculine-imaged sport, become a big-game hunter, outdoorsman, mountain climber. He may find satisfaction enough from some outlet as to have no problem at all which he is aware of as a sexual infirmity. He may be unaware of his impotence because he is blinded by his dazzling success and superiority in another field.

But in his quest for confirmation of his masculinity, a quest which he usually perceives as a search for sexual satisfaction and new conquests, his attention is attracted, with the force of the pull of gravity, to the potent Bodies in the classes beneath him, to the strength. He may sexually exploit the white-collar Bodies at the office; then, on his descent toward the Power Source, he may be drawn to the blue-collar Bodies in the plant. If these Bodies leave him still in the clutches of his lust and insecurity, he will bore deeper and deeper into the lower strata until he finds his sexual Balm of Gilead. There is a Pandora's box of sexual aberrations here.

The Body is tropical, warm, hot: Fire! It is soft,

pleasing to the touch, luscious to the kiss. The blood is hot. Muscles are strength. *The basic motion of the women of the elite is flight from their bodies.* The weakness of the female body when contrasted to the strength of the male body is an obvious attribute of femininity as manifested in social imagery. Thus, to enhance and emphasize the femininity of her image – which is mandatory in order that she present a sharp feminine contrast to the effeminate image of her man, the Omnipotent Administrator – she seeks to increase the weakness of her body and stamp out all traces of strength, to differentiate it further from the effeminate form of her man. An appearance of strength in her body is called *ugly*.

Having projected her strength, her domestic component, on to the women beneath her, she achieves an image of frailty, weakness, helplessness, delicacy, daintiness. Silks, ruffles, frills, bangles, and laces are her element. In the realm of sex, because the act of sexual intercourse is both a physical and mental process, a joint venture between the Mind and the Body, her basic contradiction is that she is physically inadequate while mentally voracious, with her mind in extreme conflict with her body. The mechanism of her orgasm, which begins in her body and ends in the psychic depths of her mind, becomes short-circuited in the struggle between her mind and her body.

Sitting at the foot of her bed, like the mute Sphinx on the bank of the Nile, is the Ogre of Frigidity. She is terrified, because of the quality of her life, by the prospect of becoming a life-termer in the prison of frigidity. Her basic fear is frigidity, the state in which her frantic search for Ultrafemininity collides with an icepack death of the soul : where the fire in her body is extinguished by the ice in her mind. The psychic core of her sensuality, the male-seeking pole of her Female Principle, the trigger of the mechanism of her orgasm, moves beyond the reach or range of the effeminate clitoris of her man. Frigid, cold, icy, ice. Arctic. Antarctic. At the end of her flight from her body is a sky-high wall of ice. (If a lesbian is anything she is a frigid woman, a frozen cunt, with a warp and a crack in the wall of her ice.)

In proportion to the intensity of the Ultrafeminine's fear and feel of the ice is her psychic lust for the flame, for the heat of the fire : the Body. The Ultrafeminine, seeking sexual satisfaction, finds only physical exhaustion in the bed of the Omnipotent Administrator, and the odds are against her finding psychic satisfaction there. Her 'psychic bridegroom' is the Supermasculine Menial. The Omnipotent Administrator, having repudiated and abdicated his body, his masculine component which he has projected on to the men beneath him, cannot present his woman, the Ultrafeminine, with an image of masculinity capable of penetrating into the psychic depths where the treasure of her orgasm is buried. The sexual act being a joint venture of the Mind and Body, though he satisfy her body and sap its strength, he cannot touch that magic spot in her mind which triggers the mechanism of her orgasm. Bereft of psychic satisfaction, and inhibited by social conventions and mores from embarking on a quest for her sexual fulfillment, yet performing her function as a mother and wife to the Omnipotent Administrator, the Ultrafeminine becomes a psychic celibate.

At the nth degree of the Ultrafeminine's scale of psychic lust (the contours of which few men or women throughout their entire lives ever in fact explore, resort being had to the forms of sublimation) stands the walking phallus symbol of the Supermasculine Menial. Though she may never have had a sexual encounter with a Supermasculine Menial, she is fully convinced that he can fulfill her physical need. It will be no big thing for him to do since he can handle those Amazons down there with him, with his strong body, rippling muscles, his strength and fire, the driving force of his spine, the thrust of his hips and the fiery steel of his rod. But what wets the Ultra-feminine's juice is that she is allured and tortured by the secret, intuitive knowledge that he, her psychic bridegroom, can blaze through the wall of her ice, plumb her psychic depths, test the oil of her soul, melt the iceberg in her brain, touch her inner sanctum, detonate the bomb of her orgasm, and bring her sweet release.

The chip on the Supermasculine Menial's shoulder is the fact that he has been robbed of his mind. In an uncannily effective manner, the society in which he lives has assumed in its very structure that he, minus a mind, is the embodiment of Brute Power. The bias and reflex of the society are against the cultivation or even the functioning of his mind, and it is borne in upon him from all sides that the society is actually deaf, dumb, and blind to his mind. The products of his mind, unless they are very closely associated with his social function of Brute Power, are resented and held in contempt by society as a whole. The further away from Brute Power his mental productions stand, the more emphatically will they be rejected and scorned by society, and treated as upstart invasions of the realm of the Omnipotent Administrator. His thoughts count for nothing. He doesn't run, regulate, control, or administer anything. Indeed, he is himself regulated, manipulated, and controlled by the Omnipotent Administrators. The struggle of his life is for the emancipation of his mind, to receive recognition for the products of his mind, and official recognition of the fact that he has a mind.

In his society, the Mind has been adjudged superior to the Body, and he knows that he is the Body and the Omnipotent Administrator is the Mind. It's Mind over matter, and the Body is matter. He may despise the Omnipotent Administrator for his physical weakness and envy him for his mind; or he may despise his own body and idolize the weak body of the Omnipotent Administrator. He may even strive to attain a weak physical image himself in order to identify with the image of the Omnipotent Administrator. The people at the base of society, where the Supermasculine Menial is, are well known for the reflex of attempting to conform to the style, pattern, manners, and habits of the upper classes, of the Omnipotent Administrators and Ultrafeminines. Just how this works itself out is a problem for analysis by sociologists and social psychologists on the mass level, and the headshrinkers and nutcrackers on the individual level. What we are outlining here is a perspective from which such analysis might best be approached.

The psychic bride of the Supermasculine Menial is the Ultrafeminine. She is his 'dream girl'. She, the delicate, weak, helpless Ultrafeminine, exerts a magnetic attraction upon him. When he compares her with his own woman, the strong, self-reliant Amazon, lust for her burns in his brain. He recoils from the excess of strength injected into the Amazon by the Domestic Function she performs. Also, since standards of beauty are set by the elite, the Ultrafeminine personifies the official standard of feminine beauty of society as a whole. Influenced by and imbued with this official standard of beauty, while at the same time surrounded by Amazons who do not embody this standard and who are in fact clashing with it, the Supermasculine Menial develops an obsessive yearning and lust for sexual contact with the Ultrafeminine. These yearnings are compounded by the fact that on the whole they are foredoomed to remain unfulfilled. The society has arranged things so that the Supermasculine Menial and the Ultrafeminine are not likely to have access or propinquity to each other conducive to stimulating sexual involvement. In fact, it has not been rare for the Supermasculine Menial and the Ultrafeminine to be severely persecuted, if not put to death, for such sexual contact.

The Amazon is in a peculiar position. Just as her man has been deprived of his manhood, so she has been deprived of her full womanhood. Society has decreed that the Ultrafeminine, the woman of the elite, is the goddess on the pedestal. The Amazon is the personification of the rejected domestic component, the woman on whom 'dishpan hands' seem not out of character. The worship and respect which both the Omnipotent Administrator and the Supermasculine Menial lavish upon the image of the Ultrafeminine is a source of deep vexation to the Amazon. She envies the pampered, powderpuff existence of the Ultrafeminine and longs to incorporate these elements into her own life. Alienated from the feminine component of her nature, her reinforced domestic component is an awesome burden and shame of which she longs to be free.

The Amazon finds it difficult to respect the Supermasculine Menial. She sees him essentially as only half a man, an incomplete man. Having no sovereignty over himself, he hasn't that sovereignty over her which our traditional patriarchal myths lead her to believe he should have. On a still deeper level, the urges and needs of the Amazon's psyche move her toward the source of power, toward the receptacle of sovereignty – an attraction motivated by the Primeval Urge to transcend the Primeval Mitosis. When the Primeval Sphere split into the male and female hemispheres, the attribute of sovereignty was reposited in the male hemisphere, and this attribute exercises a magnetic attraction upon the female hemisphere. Usurping the Supermasculine Menial's mind, the Omnipotent Administrator usurped all sovereignty; and because of his monopoly on sovereignty, he is the psychic bridegroom of the Amazon. In another sense, however, being also attracted to the body of the Supermasculine Menial, the Amazon is lost between two worlds.

In net effect, then, there will exist in Class Society two sets of competing images. Contending for the crown of masculinity is one image based on the Body and another based on the Mind; contending for the crown of femininity is one image based on weak, helpless Ultrafemininity and another based on the strong, self-reliant attributes of the Amazon. In a society with a racially homogeneous population, in which the people at the top are racially the same as the ones at the bottom, the competing images are not mutually exclusive. A Supermasculine Menial, for instance, who acquires the training of an Omnipotent Administrator, can become a member of the elite and function accordingly – assuming the existence of some vertical social mobility, which is not, of course, always the case. But even if he is prevented from ascending the social ladder in fact, a Supermasculine Menial can at least imagine himself doing so without first having to transcend any biological barriers. Likewise, an Omnipotent Administrator can descend the social ladder, develop his muscles, and hoe the row with the coolest serf on the manor. The women, too, can descend or ascend, depending on the merits, without having to breach a biological chain.

But in a society where there exists a racial caste system, where the people at the top are sharply distinguished from those at the bottom by race as well as social image, then the two sets of competing images can come to be considered mutually exclusive. The gulf between the Mind and the Body will seem to coincide with the gulf between the two races. At that point, the fear of biological miscegenation is transposed into social imagery; and since the distinction between the two races is founded in biology, the social distinction between Mind and Body is made sacred. Any attempt by the Supermasculine Menial to heal his wound and reclaim his mind will be viewed as a malignant desire to transcend the laws of nature by mixing, 'mongrelizing', miscegenating. Coming from the other side, if a member of the elite should attempt to bridge the gulf, it will be conceived as the rankest form of degeneracy and treason to caste. Deep-seated fears and emotions, which are in fact connected with biological traits and are part of a mechanism to aid racial and ethnic survival, are harnessed to social images and thereby transformed into weapons of the Class Struggle. Race fears are weapons in the struggle between the Omnipotent Administrator and the Supermasculine Menial for control of sexual sovereignty.

The Supermasculine Menial and the Amazon are the least alienated from the biological chain, although

their minds – especially the Supermasculine Menials'!
– are in a general state of underdevelopment. Still,
they are the wealth of a nation, an abundant supply
of unexhausted, unde-essenced human raw material
upon which the future of the society depends and
with which, through the implacable march of history
to an ever broader base of democracy and equality,
the society will renew and transform itself.

CONVALESCENCE

... just as in childhood I envied Negroes for what seemed to me their superior masculinity, so I envy them today for what seems to me their superior physical grace and beauty. I have come to value physical grace very highly, and I am now capable of aching with all my being when I watch a Negro couple on the dance floor, or a Negro playing baseball or basketball. *They are on the kind of terms with their own bodies that I should like to be on with mine, and for that precious quality they seem blessed to me.* [Italics added.]

> Norman Podhoretz: 'My Negro Problem – And Ours',
> *Commentary*, February 1963

Why envy the Negro his grace, his physical skills? Why not ask what it is that prevents grace and physical skill from becoming a general property of the young? Mr Podhoretz speaks of middle-class, white respectability – what does this mean but being cut off from the labor process, the work process, the creative process, as such? *The solution is thus not the direct liquidation of the color line, through the liquidation of color; but rather through a greater physical connectedness of the whites; and a greater intellective connectedness of the blacks ...'* [Italics added.]

> Irving Louis Horowitz, Chairman,
> Department of Sociology. Hobart and William Smith Colleges,
> Geneva, New York, *Commentary*, June 1963

If the separation of the black and white people in America along the color line had the effect, in terms of social imagery, of separating the Mind from the Body – the oppressor whites usurping sovereignty by monopolizing the Mind, abdicating the Body and becoming bodiless Omnipotent Administrators and Ultrafeminines; and the oppressed blacks, divested of sovereignty and therefore of Mind, manifesting the Body and becoming mindless Supermasculine Menials and Black Amazons – if this is so, then the 1954 U.S. Supreme Court decision in the case of *Brown* v. *Board of Education*, demolishing the principle of segregation of the races in public education and striking at the very root of the practice of segregation generally, was a major surgical operation performed by nine men in black robes on the racial Maginot Line which is imbedded as deep as sex or the lust for lucre in the schismatic American psyche. This piece of social surgery, if successful, performed without benefit of any anesthetic except God and the Constitution, in a land where God is dead and the Constitution has been in a coma for 180 years, is more marvelous than a successful heart transplant would be, for it was meant to graft the nation's Mind back on to its Body and vice versa.

If the foregoing is true, then the history of America in the years following the pivotal Supreme Court edict should be a record of the convalescence of the nation. And upon investigation we should be able to see the Omnipotent Administrators and Ultrafeminines grappling with their unfamiliar and alienated Bodies, and the Supermasculine Menials and Amazons attempting to acquire and assert *a mind of their own*. The record, I think, is clear and unequivocal. The bargain which seems to have been struck is that the whites have had to turn to the blacks for a clue on how to swing with the Body, while the blacks have had to turn to the whites for the secret of the Mind. It was Chubby Checker's mission, bearing the Twist as *good news*, to teach the whites, whom history had taught to forget, how to shake their asses again. It is a skill they surely must once have possessed but which they abandoned for puritanical dreams of escaping the corruption of the flesh, by leaving the terrors of the Body to the blacks.

In the swift, fierce years since the 1954 school desegregation decision, a rash of seemingly unrelated mass phenomena has appeared on the American scene – deviating radically from the prevailing Hot-Dog-and-Malted-Milk norm of the bloodless, square, superficial, faceless Sunday-Morning atmosphere that was suffocating the nation's soul. And all of this in a nation where the so-called molders of public opinion, the writers, politicians, teachers, and cab drivers, are willful, euphoric liars or zip-dam ostriches and owls, a clique of undercover ghosts, a bunch of Walter Jenkinses, a lot of coffee-drinking, cigarette-smoking, sly, suck-assing, status-seeking, cheating, nervous, dry-balled, tranquillizer-gulched, countdown-minded, out-of-style, slithering snakes. No wonder that many 'innocent people', the manipulated and the stimulated, some of whom were game for a reasonable amount of mystery and even adventure, had their minds scrambled. These observers were not equipped to either *feel* or *know* that a radical break, a revolutionary leap out of their sight, had taken place in the secret parts of this nation's soul. It was as if a driverless vehicle were speeding through the American night down an unlighted street toward a stone wall and was boarded on the fly by a stealthy ghost with a drooling leer on his face, who, at the last detour before chaos and disaster, careened the vehicle down a smooth highway that leads to the future and life; and to ask these Americans to understand that they were the passengers on this driverless vehicle and that the lascivious ghost was the Saurday-night crotchfunk of the Twist,

143

or the 'Yeah, Yeah, Yeah!' which the Beatles high-jacked from Ray Charles, to ask these Calvinistic pro-fligates to see the logical and reciprocal links is more cruel than asking a hope-to-die Okie Music buff to cop the sounds of John Coltrane.

In the beginning of the era came a thief with a seven-year itch who knew that the ostriches and the owls had been bribed with a fix of Euphony, which is their kick. The thief knew that he need not wait for the cover of night, that with impunity he could show his face in the market-place in the full light of the sun, do his deed, scratch his dirt, sell his loot to the fence while the ostriches and owls, coasting on Euphony, one with his head in a hole – any hole – and the other with his head in the clouds, would only cluck and whisper and hear-see-speak no evil.

So Elvis Presley came, strumming a weird guitar and wagging his tail across the continent, ripping off fame and fortune as he scrunched his way, and, like a latter-day Johnny Appleseed, sowing seeds of a new rhythm and style in the white souls of the white youth of America, whose inner hunger and need was no longer satisfied with the antiseptic white shoes and whiter songs of Pat Boone. 'You can do anything,' sang Elvis to Pat Boone's white shoes, 'but don't you step on my Blue Suede Shoes!'

During this period of ferment and beginnings, at about the same time that the blacks of Montgomery, Alabama, began their historic bus boycott (giving birth to the leadership of Martin Luther King, signifying to the nation that, with this initiative, this first affirm-ative step, somewhere in the universe a gear in the machinery had shifted), something, a target, came into focus. The tensions in the American psyche had torn a fissure in the racial Maginot Line and through this fissure, this tiny bridge between the Mind and Body, the black masses, who had been silent and somnolent since the 'twenties and 'thirties, were now making a break toward the dimly seen light that beckoned to them through the fissure. The fact that these blacks could now take such a step was perceived by the ostriches and owls as a sign of national decay, a sign that the System had caved in at that spot. And this gave birth to a fear, a fear that quickly became a focus for all the anxieties and exasperations in the Omnipotent Administrators' minds; and to embody this perceived decay and act as a lightning rod for the fear, the beatniks bloomed on to the American scene.

Like pioneers staking their claims in the no-man's land that lay along the racial Maginot Line, the beatniks, like Elvis Presley before them, dared to do in the light of day what America had long been doing in the sneak-thief anonymity of night – consorted on a human level with the blacks. Reviled, cursed, held in contempt by the 'molders of public opinion', persecuted by the police, made into an epithet of derision by the deep-frozen geeks of the Hot-Dog-and-Malted-Milk set, the beatniks irreverently refused to go away. Allen Ginsberg and Jack Kerouac ('the Suzuki rhythm boys', James Baldwin called them, derisively, in a moment of panic, 'tired of white ambitions' and 'dragging themselves through the Negro street at dawn looking for an angry fix'; 'with', as Mailer put it, 'the black man's code to fit their facts'). Bing Crosbyism, Perry Comoism, and Dinah Shoreism had led to cancer, and the vanguard of the white youth knew it.

And as the spirit of revolt crept across the continent from that wayward bus in Montgomery, Alabama, seeping like new life into the cracks and nooks of the northern ghettos and sweeping in furious gales across the campuses of southern Negro colleges, erupting, finally, in the sit-ins and freedom rides – as this swirling maelstrom of social change convulsed the nation, shocking an unsuspecting American public, folk music, speaking of fundamental verities, climbed slowly out of the grave; and the hip lobe of the national ear, twitching involuntarily at first, began to listen.

From the moment that Mrs Rosa Parks, in that bus in Montgomery, Alabama, resisted the Omnipotent Administrator, contact, however fleeting, had been made with the lost sovereignty – the Body had made contact with its Mind – and the shock of that contact sent an electric current throughout this nation, traversing the racial Maginot Line and striking fire in the hearts of the whites. The wheels began to turn, the thaw set in, and though Emmett Till and Mack Parker were dead, though Eisenhower sent troops to Little Rock, though Autherine Lucy's token presence at the University of Alabama was a mockery – notwithstanding this, it was already clear that the 1954 major surgical operation had been successful and the patient would live. The challenge loomed on the horizon: Africa, black, enigmatic, and hard-driving, had begun to parade its newly freed nations into the U.N.; and the Islam of Elijah Muhammad, amplified as it was fired in salvos from the piercing tongue of Malcolm X, was racing through the Negro streets with Allen Ginsberg and Jack Kerouac.

Then, as the verbal revolt of the black masses soared to a cacophonous peak – the Body, the Black Amazons and Supermasculine Menials, becoming conscious, shouting, in a thousand different ways, *'I've got a Mind of my own!'*; and as the senator from

Massachusetts was saving the nation from the Strange-love grasp of Dirty Dick, injecting, as he emerged victorious, a new and vivacious spirit into the people with the style of his smile and his wife's hairdo; then, as if a signal had been given, as if the Mind had shouted to the Body, 'I'm ready!' – the Twist, super-seding the Hula Hoop, burst upon the scene like a nuclear explosion, sending its fallout of rhythm into the Minds and Bodies of the people. The fallout: the Hully Gully, the Mashed Potato, the Dog, the Smashed Banana, the Watusi, the Frug, the Swim. The Twist was a guided missile, launched from the ghetto into the very heart of suburbia. The Twist succeeded, as politics, religion, and law could never do, in writing in the heart and soul what the Supreme Court could only write on the books. The Twist was a form of therapy for a convalescing nation. The Omnipotent Administrator and the Ultrafeminine responded so dramatically, in stampede fashion, to the Twist pre-cisely because it afforded them the possibility of reclaiming their Bodies again after generations of alienated and disembodied existence.

The stiff, mechanical Omnipotent Administrators and Ultrafeminines presented a startling spectacle as they entered in droves on to the dance floors to learn how to Twist. They came from every level of society, from top to bottom, writhing pitifully though gamely about the floor, feeling exhilarating and soothing new sensations, release from some unknown prison in which their Bodies had been encased, a sense of free-dom they had never known before, a feeling of com-munion with some mystical root-source of life and vigor, from which sprang a new awareness and enjoyment of the flesh, a new appreciation of the possibilities of their Bodies. They were swinging and

gyrating and shaking their dead little asses like petri-
fied zombies trying to regain the warmth of life, re-
kindle the dead limbs, the cold ass, the stone heart, the
stiff, mechanical, disused joints with the spark of
life.

This spectacle truly startled many Negroes, because
they perceived it as an intrusion by the Mind into the
province of the Body, and this intimated chaos; because the Negroes knew, from the survival experience
of their everyday lives, that the system within which
they were imprisoned was based upon the racial
Maginot Line and that the cardinal sin, crossing the
line – which was, in their experience, usually initiated
from the black side – was being committed, en masse,
by the whites. The Omnipotent Administrators and
Ultrafeminines were storming the Maginot Line! A
massive assault had been launched without parallel
in American history, and to Negroes it was confusing.
Sure, they had witnessed it on an individual scale:
they had seen many ofays destroy the Maginot Line
in themselves. But this time it had all the appearances
of a national movement. There were even rumors that
President Kennedy and his Jackie were doing the Twist
secretly in the White House; that their Number One
Boy had been sent to the Peppermint Lounge in disguise to learn how to Twist, and he in turn brought
the trick back to the White House. These Negroes
knew that something fundamental had changed.

'Man, what done got into them ofays?' one asked.

'They trying to get back,' said another.

'Shit,' said a young Negro who made his living by
shoplifting. 'If you ask me, I think it must be the
end of the world.'

'Oooo-weee!' said a Negro musician who had been
playing at a dance and was now standing back check-

ing the dancers. 'Baby, I don't dig this action at all!
Look here, baby, pull my coat to what's going down!
I mean, have I missed it somewhere? Where've I
been? Baby, I been blowing all my life and I ain't
never dug no happenings like this. You know what,
man, I'm gon' cut that fucking weed aloose. Oooo-
weee! Check that little bitch right there! What the
fuck she trying to do? Is she trying to shake it or
break it? Oooo-weee!'

A Negro girl said: 'Take me home, I'm sick!'

Another one said: 'No, let's stay! This is too
much!'

And a bearded Negro cat, who was not interested
in learning how to Twist himself, who felt that if he
was interested in doing it, he could get up from the
table right now and start Twisting, he said, sitting at
the table with a tinsel-minded female: 'It ain't nothing. They just trying to get back, that's all.'

'Get back?' said the girl, arching her brows
quizzically. 'Get back from where?'

'From wherever they've been,' said the cat, 'where
else?'

'Are they doing it in Mississippi is what I want to
know,' said a tall, deadly-looking Negro who had a
long razor line down his left cheek and who had left
Mississippi in a hurry one night.

And the dancers: they were caught up in a whirl of
ecstasy, swinging like pendulums, mechanical like
metronomes or puppets on invisible strings being manipulated by a master with a sick sense of humor. 'They
look like Chinese doing communal exercise,' said a
Negro. 'That's all they're doing, calisthenics!'

'Yeah,' said his companion. 'They're trying to get in
shape.'

But if at first it was funny and confusing, it was

none the less a breakthrough. The Omnipotent Administrators and Ultrafeminines were discovering new aspects of the Body, new possibilities of rhythm, new ways to move. The Hula Hoop had been a false start, a mechanized, theatrical attempt by the Mind to supply to itself what only the Body can give. But, with the Twist, at last they knew themselves to be swinging. The forces acting upon the world stage in our era had created, in the collective psyche of the Omnipotent Administrators and Ultrafeminines, an irresistible urge – to just stand up and shake the ice and cancer out of their alienated white asses – and the Hula Hoop and Twist offered socially acceptable ways to do it.

Of course, not all the whites took part in these joyful experiments. For many, the more 'suggestive' a dance became – i.e., the more it became pure Body and less Mind – the more scandalous it seemed to them; and their reaction in this sense was an index to the degree of their alienation from their Bodies. But what they condemned as a sign of degeneracy and moral decay was actually a sign of health, a sign of hope for full recovery. As Norman Mailer prophesied:
' ... the Negro's equality would tear a profound shift into the psychology, the sexuality, and the moral imagination of every white alive.' Precisely because the Mind will have united with the Body, theory will have merged with practice.

It is significant that the Twist and the Hula Hoop came into the scene in all their fury at the close of the Eisenhower and the dawn of the Kennedy era. It could be interpreted as a rebellion against the vacuous Eisenhower years. It could also be argued that the same collective urge that gave rise to the Twist also swept Kennedy into office. I shudder to think that, given the closeness of the final vote in 1960, Richard Nixon might have won the election in a breeze if he had persuaded one of his Ultrafeminine daughters, not to mention Ultrapat, to do the Twist in public. Not if Kennedy had stayed on the phone a week sympathizing with Mrs Martin Luther King, Jr, over the fact that the cat was in jail, would he have won. Even as I am convinced that Luci Baines Johnson, dancing the Watusi in public with Killer Joe Piro, won more votes for her old man in 1964 than a whole boxcar full of his hog-calling speeches ever did.

When the Birmingham Revolt erupted in the summer of 1963 and President Kennedy stepped into the void and delivered his unprecedented speech to the nation on civil rights and sent his bill to Congress, the foundation had been completed. Martin Luther King, Jr, giving voice to the needs of the Body, and President Kennedy, speaking out the needs of the Mind, made contact on that day. The Twisters, sporting their blue suede shoes, moved beyond the ghost in white shoes who ate a Hot Dog and sipped Malted Milk as he danced the mechanical jig of Satan on top of Medgar Evers' tomb. In vain now would the murderers bomb that church and slaughter grotesquely those four little black girls (what did they hope to kill? were they striking at the black of the skin or the fire of the soul? at history? at the Body?). In vain also the assassins' bullets that crashed through the head of John Kennedy, taking a life, yes, but creating a larger-than-life and failing utterly to expunge from the record the March on Washington and its truth: that this nation – bourgeois or not, imperialist or not, murderous or not, ugly or not – its people, somewhere in their butchered and hypocritical souls, still contained an epic potential of spirit which is its hope, a bottomless potential which fires the imaginations of its youth. It was all too late. It was too late because it was time for the blacks ('I've got a *Mind* of my own!') to riot, to sweep through the Harlem night like a wave of locusts, breaking, screaming, bleeding, laughing, crying, rejoicing, celebrating, in a jubilee of destruction, to regurgitate the white man's bullshit they'd been eating for four hundred years; smashing the windows of the white man's stores, throwing bricks they wished were bombs, running, leaping, whirling like a cyclone through the white man's Mind, past his backlash, through the night streets of Rochester, New Jersey, Philadelphia. And even though the opposition, gorging on Hot Dogs and Malted Milk, with blood now splattered over the white shoes, would still strike out in the dark against the manifestations of the turning, showing the protocol of Southern Hospitality reserved for Niggers and Nigger Lovers – S C H W E R N E R – C H A N E Y – G O O D M A N – it was still too late. For not only had Luci Baines Johnson danced the Watusi in public with Killer Joe, but the Beatles were on the scene, injecting Negritude by the ton into the whites, in this post-Elvis Presley-beatnik era of ferment.

Before we toss the Beatles a homosexual kiss – saying, 'If a man be ass enough to reach for the bitch in them, that man will kiss a man, and if a woman reaches for the stud in them, that woman will kiss a woman' – let us marvel at the genius of their image, which comforts the owls and ostriches in the one spot where Elvis Presley bummed their kick: Elvis, with his *unfunky* (yet mechanical, alienated) bumpgrinding, was still too much Body (too soon) for the strained collapsing psyches of the Omnipotent Administrators and Ultrafeminines; whereas the Beatles, affecting the caucasoid crown of femininity and ignoring the Body on the visual plane (while their music on the contrary being full of Body), assuaged the doubts of the owls and ostriches by presenting an incorporeal, cerebral image.

Song and dance are, perhaps, only a little less old than man himself. It is with his music and dance, the recreation through art of the rhythms suggested by and implicit in the tempo of his life and cultural environment, that man purges his soul of the tensions of daily strife and maintains his harmony in the universe. In the increasingly mechanized, automated, cybernated environment of the modern world – a cold, bodiless world of wheels, smooth plastic surfaces, tubes, pushbuttons, transistors, computers, jet propulsion, rockets to the moon, atomic energy – man's need for affirmation of his biology has become that much more intense. He feels need for a clear definition of where his body ends and the machine begins, where man ends and the *extensions* of man begin. This great mass hunger, which transcends national or racial boundaries, recoils from the subtle subversions of the mechanical environment which modern technology is creating faster than man, with his present savage relationship to his fellow men, is able to receive and assimilate. This is the central contradiction of the twentieth century; and it is against this backdrop that America's attempt to unite its Mind with its Body, to save its soul, is taking place.

It is in this connection that the blacks, personifying the Body and thereby in closer communion with their biological roots than other Americans, provide the saving link, the bridge between man's biology and man's machines. In its purest form, as adjustment to the scientific and technological environment of our era, as purgative and lullaby-soother of man's soul, it is the jazz issuing from the friction and harmony of the American Negro with his environment that captured the beat and tempo of our times. And although modern science and technology are the same whether in New York, Paris, London, Accra, Cairo, Berlin, Moscow, Tokyo, Peking, or São Paulo, jazz is the only true international medium of communication current in the world today, capable of speaking creatively, with equal intensity and relevance, to the people in all those places.

The less sophisticated (but no less Body-based) popular music of urban Negroes – which was known as Rhythm and Blues before the whites appropriated and distilled it into a product they called Rock 'n Roll – is the basic ingredient, the core, of the gaudy, cacophonous hymns with which the Beatles of Liverpool drive their hordes of Ultrafeminine fans into catatonia and hysteria. For Beatle fans, having been alienated from their own Bodies so long and so deeply, the effect of these potent, erotic rhythms is electric. Into this music, the Negro projected – as it were, *drained off*, as pus from a sore – a powerful sensuality, his pain and lust, his love and his hate, his ambition and his despair. The Negro projected into his music his very Body. The Beatles, the four long-haired lads from Liverpool, are offering up as their gift the Negro's Body, and in so doing establish a rhythmic communication between the listener's own Mind and Body.

Enter the Beatles – soul by proxy, middlemen between the Mind and the Body. A long way from Pat Boone's White Shoes. A way station on a slow route traveled with all deliberate speed.

THE AUTHOR

Eldridge Cleaver was born in Little Rock, Arkansas, in 1935. In 1958 he was sentenced to thirteen years in prison for attempted murder, serving nine years in the California state prisons of San Quentin, Folsom and Soledad before his release on parole in 1966. A collection of essays written while in prison, *Soul on Ice* became one of the surprise international bestsellers of 1968 and was awarded the Martin Luther King Memorial Prize. Declaring himself to be 'a full-time revolutionary in the struggle for black liberation in America', he joined the militant Black Panther Party and was made Minister of Information. He was the Peace and Freedom Party's Presidential candidate in the 1968 U.S. elections. Then in November 1968, just as he was due to return to prison after the revocation of his parole, Cleaver went underground. He reappeared, first in Cuba and then in Algiers, where he still lives. A collection of post-prison writings and speeches was published in 1969 under the title *Eldridge Cleaver*; the transcript of an interview by Lee Lockwood in Algiers, *Conversation with Eldridge Cleaver*, appeared in 1971.

CAPE EDITIONS